Praise for *In, and Of*, by Jack Haas

"...an enthralling, true-life account... Because of its philosophical, emotional, and insightful narrative, *In, and Of* is very strongly recommended reading for students of metaphysics and the contemplative life." *The Midwest Book Review* (Reviewer's Choice)

"...an embarrassment of riches... one of the best books I've ever read." George Fisk (Cosmic Concepts Press publisher)

"...a poetic and stunning piece of work that will leave you inspired to contemplate your own existence in this world. ...Jack Haas has quite a tale to tell." Nancy Jackson (*Dog-Eared Book Reviews*)

"...lucid...and uncompromising. ...Read in awe." Benjamin Tucker (author of *Roadeye*)

Praise for *The Way of Wonder*, by Jack Haas

"...written out of reverence for the beauty in all life. ...especially recommended reading for students of comparative religion and personal spirituality." *The Midwest Book Review*

"...a most unusual, and powerful book." George Fisk (author of *A New Sense of Destiny*)

"Wow! ...What a glorious, uplifting, inspiring affirmation it is!" Jonathon Kerslake (editor, *Lived Experience*)

"This book really impressed me. ... a most stimulating read." Alicia Karen Elkins (*Gotta Write Network Reviews*)

Copyright© 2003 Jack Haas

All rights reserved. No part of this publication may be reproduced or transmitted in any form or by any means, electronic or mechanical, including photocopying, recording, or by any information storage or retrieval system, without written permission from the Publisher, except in quoting brief passages.

Thanks to Maggie McGhee, Tanis Mager, and Benjamin Tucker, for their generous and genius editing comments.

Library of Canada Cataloguing in Publication data:

Haas, Jack, 1966-
  Roots and wings : adventures of a spirit on earth / Jack Haas.

  ISBN 0-9731007-4-5

  1. Haas, Jack, 1966- 2. Authors, Canadian (English)--Biography.* I. Title.
  PS8565.A145Z53 2003   C818'.609   C2003-910425-7
  PR9199.4.H32Z47 2003

Published by Iconoclast Press, Vancouver, BC, and Hilo, HI.
Head Office
Suite 144
3495 Cambie St.
Vancouver, BC.
V5Z 4R3
Canada

admin@iconoclastpress.com
website: www.iconoclastpress.com

Cover photo by Tanis Mager.

For my mother,
whose soul gave ground for roots,
and whose love gave space for wings.

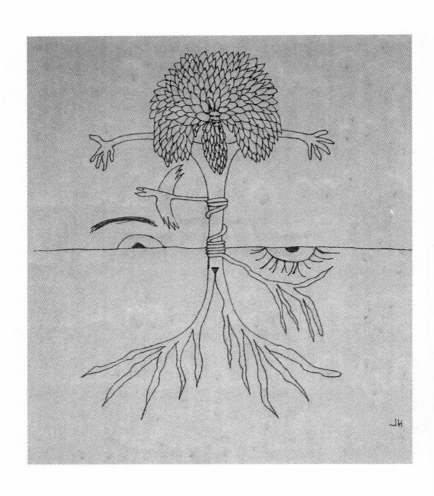

THE TREE OF LIFE
Illustration by the author

PART 1:
COURTING THE MOTHER

*"Today I am proud to say that I am **inhuman**, that I belong not to men and governments, that I have nothing to do with creeds and principles. I have nothing to do with the creaking machinery of humanity- I belong to the earth! ...We have no need for genius- genius is dead. We have need for strong hands, for spirits who are willing to give up the ghost and put on flesh..."*
Henry Miller

"But on the human plane that would have been destruction: living life instead of living one's own life is forbidden. It is a sin to go into divine matter. And that sin has an inexorable punishment: the person who dares go into that secret, in losing her individual life, disorganizes the human world."
Clarice Lispector

one

Out in this world, in this impossible world, in this crazy, mysterious, magical world. Out into this world I came, like a wild thought fleeing its captor. Out and out I plunged, never towards but only away, as if I was born solely to become what God had not yet made. As if life was my way to expand the miracle, to make it more than it is or has been, and to seed that new realm even though I was lurching forward with all the grace of a limping man in a blinding sand storm, who yet was filled with all the privilege of a knight sent in pursuit of the Grail, because I was a seeker and I was the sought, and yet there was nothing to find in life that was better than creating what had not yet been.

To do this is to embrace the making instead of the made, and so to serve the Self like a polished magnifying glass making focused light of the giving sun. To be one with the Creator is to have entered into the stillness of the living word become flesh, and to be that living flesh also; it is to be the gold which is not gold but rather the condensed light of God formed out of the archetypical blueprint and into the eternal liquid structure of the ephemeral day.

And for this have I lived in our implausible world as if on an endless tightrope strung between the pinnacles of confusion and wonder, while hovering over an infinite abyss as full of joy as it is of sorrow. For there was a time when the yin and the yang, if there be such divisions, were stretched apart to their furthest dimensions within me, leaving my mind in the lofty reaches, and my heart in the pit of hell, so that I was ripped open by the insoluble feud between them. Which is why it seemed that nothing worked, because I was composed of two perfect halves, but I was not whole, and since the agony came with the ecstasy, the tug-of-war between the two halves became the goad and the leash from which I sprang forth only then to be hauled back again with ignoble regularity. And thus I was forced out into life, to take it in, enjoy it, despise it, correct it, and destroy it, and was then pulled painfully back again, withdrawn so as not to be petted nor fed. As if to enter the banquet, to drool a bit, and then be pushed quickly out the other side, in a neverending chain of engagements, was my destiny, so as to live and to not live, to die and to not die, and to always be given and never to have, which was the only way I could learn how to not-exist while existing, to enter the jail without being taken prisoner, and to fly without growing wings, so that in the end I could live free upon this earth only by continually wriggling out of my old self, and becoming what I had never been.

It was this pendulous oscillation, which in its singular turn drove me nearer to myself by the same distance it tore me apart, that broke and also mended me together. How else could I describe it? How else could it describe me? Others called it life. I didn't know what to call it. It was all very strange. Very, very strange. I never knew a damn thing. No one ever does.

And so I had to learn to embody all of my own contradictions: I had to accept and deny myself; I had to have faith in God, and I had to rebel; I had to love and also abhor the flesh; I had to strive and not strive, be and not-be, do and not-do, and take on all of life's imperfections knowing that they were somehow perfect.

I had to always be coming, and always be going. And in that provincial domain of our feral aristocracy, where the duty and dreaming mingled into an indivisible one, nobody could have told me what I would find when I ceased living with expectation, preconception, or need. No one could show me how to get no where. For throughout those formative days of my so-called separate existence, there were many seemingly inexplicable and yet undeniable preconceptions, synchronicities, exuberances, coincidences, messages, voices, wonderings, and dreams. Good God there were dreams. Night after night did I writhe upon the mythical membrane in between consciousness and sleep, where the greater and lesser forces spun webs of unspeakable drama throughout my defenseless becoming, while obstinate realities took refuge rhapsodically within me.

I did not know then what life's reckless meaning beckoned, for I recognized no impetus behind my manic actions other than flight and boredom, though I knew not why I was bored, nor what it was I fled. In fact, I did not at first seek truth, only a complacency to dispel such arduous yearnings. Every act was an escape from myself and the mind's implications. I was made stable by the force I exerted against what opposed me, and not because I could stand. And that is that.

Never let it be said, though, that my despair outweighed my euphoria, or my agony my bliss, for I have gone down into the belly of the beast, and there I howled with a woe and tremor enough to chill the gods, and there I also laughed and roared with a rapture enough to cause them envy. And there it was that I gathered up both sides of that rope strung between everything and its opposite, until I pulled the chasm into me, filled that hollow with my own emptiness, and caused my divided world to merge the darkened moon into the light of the sun.

But in order to do this I had to learn to sit with the disquiet, to feel it, accept it, and then throw up my arms in resignation, and hallelujah, for it is a crazy path which the spirit partakes in its breathtaking descent into the earth. It is a perilous dive into the catacombs of the flesh, wherein the transformations are as fast and furious as the raging seas of spirit all around. And it was only in the release of all that refuses to fall that, paradoxically, I learned again how to fly. Which is to say, it was only when I allowed fear to become

7

loneliness, loneliness to become acceptance, and acceptance to turn into wonder, that …that I became the unknown God.

This came about because, in the intimacy of all our absences, where the self assumes no borders, and form shatters without breaking, I remembered …how to forget. I forgot, and that was enough to release me from woe. For only the unadorned Self can slip through the membrane of matter and into the void of the One, because you cannot get to the other side by trying to get there, but only by letting go of what holds you, and floating away though yet planted amidst life's pervasive glue.

For me there was no other option. I had to leave, and I had to stay. And in the violent collision of these two necessities, in the wash and fire of the spirit's healing, in the sacrificial evisceration of the mind, in the fiery assumption of the grosser self, when I knew I was done for, and the Word itself hovered hopelessly above the willess flesh, at the crescendo of my dismemberment, I suddenly came to peace because I finally realized that everything in life was wrong, that it was intended to be wrong, that God was insane, that men were as devils, and that it was going to get far worse before it got any better. And, given these unequivocal suppositions, easy enough it was to recognize life as naught but a terrible joke. But, then, after all …a joke it was. So with that matured understanding it occurred to me that it is up to each one of us to choose how we take that joke- whether we walk through our days with a foul and bitter scorn, or skip merrily through life with a hearty chuckle. That is what I came upon. And what happened to me is …I began to laugh.

And in that jocular twist it seemed as if everything wrong had suddenly vanished, and the only thing to remain was …the inexplicable. And so all I was left with was a formless, passionate, intimate …faith. I have no better way to poorly describe it. All I was left with was the madness and mystery called life. And that was enough, for if truth be known, the last straw does not break the camel's back …it gives it wings. And so my cup had gone from being half empty, to being half full, and the cup which is eternally half full, is the same one which forever runneth over, for appreciation is one of the symptoms of heaven, of that terrible, agonizing gratitude, the kind that bends you over weeping and then grabs you by the breastbone and lifts you up in joy.

Gratitude. When you sift out the trials and struggles, the loneliness and perils of existence, no matter who you are or how you got there, what's left in the end is the privilege of life.

It was through that privileged and pathless mayhem that I came like the mountain wind, without warning or direction. And the curses and blame did not end nor impede me as I went on beyond the God who is and the God who is not, beyond what the powers made of

8

me and what they took away, beyond all way and connection, beyond where they caught me and where they tried to make me stay. I went on. Up, and up I climbed, to where I could not climb back down. I climbed up and up, alone and not wanting to be alone, until I chose once again to reverse my course, and took that desperate mad plunge back down, down through the sky, through the earth, through the mind, and into the soul, for though I no longer cared to be in this realm, I also cared to be here, despite the love and sadness of it all.

For that is the heart and the reason I came here. To dive in, and descend, and never look back with regret, nor with worry. For below the waters of life is the same Self, as above that wild surface.

*

two

But let me explain. Let me hopelessly explain why I cannot explain what I cannot help but try to explain.

Were it not for the fact that God dwells, and is worthy, in all people, I could not just now have so emphatically declared the gospel of my own idiosyncratic dissent, ascent, and descent. For life never follows an intended course, because there is no course here, there is only life. Here, where everyone dances their puppet-self on the ephemeral stage of Babylon; here there is no authority, there is only a ruleless dance, not danced rulelessly. Here, the sun shines, the trees twinkle, and the trumpets play Taps at a hero's funeral, and yet there is no one around to hear the music except mourners, and so it seems such a waste, because the miracle hems us in as much as it inspires us, and so the glory and grief walk hand in hand and only a fool would choose to walk along with them, and only a madman would not. And that is why it seems such a waste. Though it isn't. It just seems that way.

Most of us come into life without asking, and leave without knowing why. We laugh, strive, want, suffer, and cry. And yet there are times when life stands us back up, when life awakens us with a haunting. You see, I had lived so long within dreams of my own invention, that I had lived for so long without actually living. And then, somewhere in between it all, amongst the cacophony and the void, when the hold I had on life- or the hold life had on me- weakened as if from sublime intent ...I began to remember. And in that remembrance I forgot without caring.

Many things I will never understand nor be capable of explaining: Why we are the way we are; why life is the way it is; when it all began, and where it is all headed- of these I have not a clue. There

9

were many odd and unexpected experiences, mythical hallmarks, and sublime events throughout my journey, but, I suppose, this is the way it happens to us in this fantastic realm where being and becoming are both different and also the same, because what was is what will be, and what will be is what is, for time is a false matrix placed over a continuum, just as the acorn is the oak when seen through its continuance, and the song is the singer as long as the music goes on.

My song begins back when I was eight years old, and my family and I had moved for two months to Halifax, Nova Scotia, where my father was teaching at St. Mary's University for the summer. During our stay we met and spent a great deal of time with another family which had two sons slightly older than myself. At the end of the summer our families were departing for different areas of the continent and, on the evening in which we said our goodbyes, I lay down for bed, not knowing if I would see this family- which I had grown to love- ever again. That night I experienced something immensely powerful, awakening, and destructive. The entire night I lay awake as if in a fever, though I had no fever, yet there was a tremendous battle between two opposed paradigms, or visions, going on somewhere deep inside me. In one vision I was on a gentle conveyor-belt with many others; there was a calm and peaceful feeling, and my body was seemingly immersed in a bath of harmonious energy. Then the vision would switch, and suddenly everyone would be contorted, and off the conveyor belt, thrashing their way manically down crazed and dirty streets, struggling to go forward, but being impeded by, and impeding, the flood of insane humanity coming the other way. In this second vision there was no peace, no respite, no harmony, and my body felt as if it were flung into a chaotic electrical maelstrom from which there was no escape. Then the whole show would flip over again, and the conveyor-belt scene and peaceful feeling would take over for a while, and then back again to the chaos and disharmony, and so on, the whole night, as I was flung continually between opposites, and lay pinned to the bed, an eight-year old kid who, as best as I can say now, had just begun his inexorable, head-long fall into the flesh.

Perhaps the troubling initiation I underwent, that night in Halifax, came about because, in parting from that family which I had quickly grown to love and enjoy, I was receiving the first brutal awakening to one of life's darker characteristics- loss. I had begun to care, and, concomitantly, I had been cast out of the careless, quiescent realm of childhood, and into the trauma, confusion, and peacelessness of the flesh.

I see now that, in many ways, at eight years old I had actually not yet left the warm and protected chamber of the womb. Not until that night when the blissful glow of childhood was suddenly swept out

10

from under me, the floor beneath me vanished, and with nothing to hold onto but the insanity of the world itself, I began the terrible and essential downward plunge from limitless play, into limitless troubles.

To be sure, it is a long and agonizing descent from the untroubled firmament, out of the womb, through the mind, into the heart, and down to earth.

A close friend of mine once shared a very telling dream she had of this sense of loss which our angelic nature suffers upon arrival in the world. She had dreamt of a community of winged people, who spent their days flying joyfully together in a mountainous canyon they had come to call home. One day, however, they were all captured by humans, had their wings cut off, and then were released to live out the rest of their days without the freedom so natural to them. After this horrible mutilation some of them tried their best to assimilate themselves into the human world, though they never really belonged, and continued to carry the burden of loss and sorrow to the end of their days; others retreated from mankind, and sat up high, overlooking the canyon, forever remembering when they were all together and free to fly; and some took a last flight off of those canyon walls, not being able to endure the pain of their new imprisonment.

As I write this down shivers are flowing into me from above, and tears are struggling not to fall, which is always a good sign that I have hit upon a truth. And though I have often felt as one of those whom had their wings clipped, and have anguished over freedoms I do not even remember losing, I see now that I have not come to this earth to mourn, to suffer, or to belong. I have come so as to once again learn how to fly. And yet, as I have found during the thirty-six years I have now been in this world, it is a different thing altogether to take wing as an angel, than to soar as a man.

*

three

Coming into this world as I did, as we all do- like little God-maggots, growing in the stool and searching for our new wings that we might learn again to fly- I could never have imagined what was to happen. How could I? Who, after all, can know the unknowable? Who indeed?

It began as a vast, phantasmagoric festival of non-meaning; the Dream bloomed, charged and buoyant within me, as moments blended and engaged, became made and unmade, then ripped and mended into the fabric of our intertwined lives.

11

Real life was a harmony barely audible, through the bustle and clamor of the day, to which, however, I eventually learned to dance with wild abandon upon this seemingly dead and spiritless earth.

Like all others I was at first trapped in this cosmic pandora, roaming hard and yet hobbled by the proximity of our woes; aflame and fluid in the directionless stream, I recognized pattern and intent, though I knew not what was intended. Tangled in life's multiple cobwebs, like someone passed along the upstretched hands of an infinite crowd, I let myself be carried away by the directionless touch; touch was all that mattered, where I went was of no concern.

Like a worn vessel I listed into the seasonal winds to wherever it was I was taken, indifferently swept into the infinite storms, the love, and the doldrums.

You see, when I initially fell to this world, I did not die but was badly maimed. Broken and lost I remained like just another fallen angel, wrecked and unable to fly back to God. I was a reality, but I was not in reality, and so I realized instantly that I did not belong, that I would never belong, and that ...I was not supposed to belong. For if I belonged, how indeed could I see through the lie, the folly, and the futility of our so-called lives. I did not belong, but I belonged for that very reason. It seemed like one hell of a cruel joke.

In fact, as soon as I was spat forth onto this makeshift prison of woe and confusion, they got a hold of me, and the inevitable corruption began.

It was in a blood-thirsty land into which I was deposited without weapons, knowledge, or crime. Or so it seemed at the time. For in the beginning nothing happened but a great celestial fiasco; as the full moon itself gave light to the rainbow, the sun cast darkness upon the land, and the stars themselves shone mystic anguish in retaliation to the night. The cosmos pitched Sol versus Luna, and Luna versus Sol, but never found a solution.

In fact the whole desperate mess- of being- was like seeing something obscurely reflected in a rippling sea; above were the ethereal images, below was the ever-changing all. But that's life, after all- always reflected, always upside down, always fluid and moving.

It was into this mercurial, amniotic flow that I fell away from everything true. In perilous adhesion to the concupiscence of the day did I swim in the dark and Godless depths. Manifold points of separateness deluded me into becoming, and I drowned gleefully in the habit of being, gasping wantonly with lungs which had forgotten how to effortlessly breathe.

My inward gaze was not yet strong enough to balance out the weight of the outer show. Caught in the movement, and swept fruitlessly into the vast organic sea of human misery, I was in hopeless pain, the pain of one who belongs nowhere, because the plague of

12

mankind was everywhere, and spreading, piling up shit upon shit, until there was nowhere to walk without being soiled, nowhere to run without being chased, and nowhere to sing without being caged.

Everything I had learned from society was a malicious lie, or, at best, a cowardly act of negligence burying the miracle of life with every word, and burying the spirit and soul with pith and petty bile.

I forgive others their blindness, but I curse them for having no strength, no love, no humility.

And yet, as I found, it was not with others that my failure or victory lay, but only with myself, for I had to realize that if I allowed myself to get tangled in other's cares, or fall victim to their pleasures and desires, I would certainly miss my call.

And so, as if driving a foreign car, on foreign streets, in a foreign country, I had to learn to inhabit this foreign world- and become an invisible driver, stealthily making my way through the roadblocks, alleys, and highways of this planet of love which was somehow lousy with gloom. For I realized that most of society would do everything it could to stand in my way, everything it could to hold me back, to convince me out of my passion, out of myself, and out of life, and so I learned to depend on nothing and nobody, but only to believe in myself, for I saw that if I blamed others for my station, I gave away my power, if I sought out others for my salvation, I gave away my spirit, and if I needed others to cure my sorrow, I gave away my force.

The trick, I discovered, was to not let mankind spoil my time in this remarkable, enviable world, but to dance my own dance and pay no heed to the confusion all about me.

And yet it was an awful process, fighting my way through the false self, false perspective, and false purpose, all of which had been inculcated into my formative being by the magnanimous elders of our times. But then finally, in the quagmire of lostness, I found something I cared for more than comfort, honor, or money. And that was …myself. And as soon as I tuned in to that self I realized that my life had been like an old and beaten radio that looked worn on the outside, but man when you put the earphones on and turned it up, damn if it didn't play good music.

I could hear again the fiddler. I was opened, lifted, cleansed, moved, and dancing. And I was still.

It is so hard to describe this transformation, but somehow, unpredictably, in those vagrant, directionless wanderings, I had found within myself something's nothingness; I had stumbled unwittingly upon an indisputable recognition. I did not know what it was, I simply accepted that it was …me.

It was as if, in the last battle in the ghastly war of attrition my soul led against all lies, there was nothing left but an eye, torn out at the roots and inverted by its own intransigent sight. And it was through this eye that I found the far-off land of which I had dreamt quite often but never seen, though when I finally I turned within ...I was there.

Yea indeed, meandering guidelessly through the tunnels of decomprehension, I had found not-finding, and lost all sense of the ground. In the absence of all image I fell joyfully away from thought towards thoughtless beauty, and into the mindless upswell of the heart's conquest.

I did not actually surrender to this or that, or what have you, I simply gave up, for I had no more need to go running about everywhere. I was finished, so to speak, though not in the vogue of any metaphysical euphemism for attainment, but because I was through with the struggle, the strain, and the whole damned mess of it; because I was surely in the magician's chambers, and had in fact been there all along. I could do nothing except the only thing there was to do when there was nothing left to do- I became still. Nothing more could have been done; as if I had been chased up a closed canyon by a mighty force, there was nowhere else I could run; I was corralled by the extraordinary shepherding of being. I had no more fight left with mankind, for fighting was exactly what had imprisoned me. Thus there was no victory, and no defeat- the war just sort of ended, at which point I turned away ...and walked on home.

*

four

Before all of that which I have just written came to pass, which was before I understood that God brings all things about through us, I had to live my life out in the world. Out in this crazy, impossible, beautiful world.

And so at thirty years of age I was in Old Delhi, India- Mother India- and had been there for three months, unable to leave, because I was going mad on loneliness, Old Monk Rum, freedom, torpor, and words.

India, Mother India, a land of madness and miracles, where nothing is reasonable, and everything belongs, because in India there is no norm, no paradigm, no structure, nor concept upon which to base any idea of right or wrong, for the Mother accepts all, and is all. If you go to India and try to fit in, you never will, because no one fits in there, not even Indians. And that, I suppose, is why the Indians greet you as if you were a deity- as one for whom there is no duplicate, because to be unique is to be eternal, as eternal as God- which is why they greet you with *namasté*: I bow to the God within you.

At the time of writing this book I have been to India a number of times, and yet to this day the only word I have learned which I continue to use, besides *chai*, is *namasté*. It is a word I am still learning, and perhaps a word I will never finish learning. *Namasté*, I bow to the God within you.

It is a word which has no similarity with any salutation from the occident, and its closest approximations are the Hawaiian word *Aloha*, and the Alaskan Upik word *Chamai*, both of which have also been pathetically mistranslated into the banal English word 'hello'.

Namasté; it is a word which destroys this world, and creates another. In an instant. For, the moment we greet or part in this way, the entire fabric of the universe is re-woven and becomes an infinitely unpatterned unity where entropy and order, the sacred and profane, and the spirit and flesh are no longer opposites, for there are no opposites, and everything is singular, secular, and sacred, and all blemish is honored as a unique addition to the gyrating, cornucopic menagerie flung out from the fecund womb of ruleless creation.

When first I stepped foot on Indian soil, I felt as if I had landed on the moon. Never had I encountered a country whose impact shook me to the very core, like India. Of course, I had arrived before 1992, which meant that the Indian government was still refusing to allow any foreign products into the country- a moratorium which had been sustained for the previous forty years, as a further Ghandian step to remove all external influences, and help return the culture to its purest state, which was impossible, of course, but it provided the likes of myself with a destination which was so thoroughly unique and untainted by the rest of the world's offal, that it was, as I said, like arriving on the moon.

At that time India was an insular, inviolable, independent entity, both economically, and spiritually. Nowhere on earth was the seething chaos so uninterrupted, so organic, so thickly perfumed with the contiguous, ever-present Great Self, animating all, choreographing all, birthing all, burning all, and being all, as in India. Even unto this day, nowhere else is God so lost within the struggling microcosm, and so found within the panoramic whole.

On my first trip I had arrived both heartbroken and with a terrible fever, which is how I always seemed to arrive at any of the destinations I chose for an indefinite overseas trip, after I had said goodbye to all I had known, sundering the chords of love and malice which bound me to others, and so launching my shuttle out into the fabulous cosmos, to whirl about until landing God knows where for an unlimited length of time.

That first trip I stayed for six months, and by the time I left the mystic land, I was a part of India, and India was a part of me, and thus

15

it would be now and forever.

And so I returned again after a few years, some two decades or so beyond that psychedelic night in Halifax, and I was on one of an infinite number of dirty, crowded, and chaotic streets of Hindustan, and all of the sudden a *déjà vu* set in, and the remembrance of that long and punishing evening as an eight-year old kid came tumbling back to me, as if I had finally come full circle and was now living out the reality of that fantasy, as if the dream symbology was now being fully manifested in my life, having taken over twenty years to play itself out, falling unnoticeably, but unavoidably, out of the timeless sublime and into time and disorder, and I was far off of the conveyor belt, and had no idea how I was going to ever get back on it again, for I was in Old Delhi, thirty-years old, and living alone in a loud and dingy, cheap as they come, crumbling hotel.

No traveler stays more than a few days in Delhi, if he or she can help it. Delhi is a place to leave, not a place to stay. Only I couldn't leave. I was a writer now. And that meant I was doomed. Doomed to live even farther apart from life, doomed to have a carbuncle forever eating away at me which no one else could see. Doomed to the awe, the solitude, and the paralysis necessary so as to allow the breech word to make its way laboriously out of the birth canal of my soul and not be dead when it hit the page.

I was a midwife, a whore, and a mother to the word back then. I would wake up every morning at about 6:30 am, just as the red orb was peaking its head above the horizon. By 7:00 am I couldn't imagine how I would make it through another minute, let alone another day, for the creative act was also a destructive act, and I was caught in the living tension between birth and death. I was in the grip of a force of which I had no knowledge at the time: the force of growth, and of decay. I was growing and dying, giving birth to the new, and burying the old. I was at every moment being born, raised, seduced, invaded, impregnated, and then giving birth, raising little ones, growing old, laying down, and dying, all at every moment of every day. Caught in the redemptive fire of the soul's own apocalypse, I was being accepted and rejected, judged and released, honored and despised, deified and denied, in each breath, act, and surrender.

But then somehow I would also be swept into the eye of the hurricane, and I would come to a calm, and after recovering enough composure to venture out, I'd have a quick breakfast every morning at one of the nearby *dhabbas*, and then head back to my little cement cell, at the mosque-like Camron Lodge, in the heart of Paharganj, Old Delhi.

The first few hours I'd spend typing into my prehistoric laptop the notes I had scribbled down the day before, always building up a work, and always tearing it down. I was an artist at work and the work was myself, and like the alchemists of old, I had confused the outer

16

with the inner, imagining that I was writing, while all the while I was being written. I was in the tumbling throes of my descent into flesh. All that lies between the pages of this book is what I remember of that fall.

I suppose I took up writing because there was no other option for me as a way to exist in the world. There was not a career, occupation, or temporary job which held any interest for me. I had no desire to live by a clock, to help mankind fill the world with trash, or to saddle my unbound existence with a label or role. In other words, I was expendable, because I refused, as much as possible, to become an unwilling cog in a moribund machine.

And so writing became the only worldly activity for which I held any interest or energy. All else was merely clutter and obstruction. Though I suppose this is a natural reaction for a person like myself, and for those of a similar disposition. In fact, I once had a dream in which I was told that the vocation of art is a refuge given by God to those who are not fit for the world. And, to be sure, I was not fit for the world, not as it was anyways.

With such a critical, and categorical understanding- that writing was the one and only option for me, a spirit come down to earth, and that such a craft was the only means for me to not drift off into an ambivalent and fruitless existence, the meaninglessness of which has led so many of my brothers and sisters onto the street and its derelict ways, because that is what happens when you lose every mooring in life and float away, becoming a derelict in the caustic sea of human inhumanity- with that understanding I threw myself into the art without knowing where it would lead, but knowing that everything else would lead nowhere.

It seems like a romantic dream to imagine a young artist in a foreign country, dwelling in down-and-out hotels, smoking cigarettes, drinking *chai*, and living out the poetic nature of the soul. But that is where it ends- a romantic dream. The rest is loneliness, melancholy, or uncertainty. And yet, what in life is that much different?

Life includes pain, and that is that. Show me a person who has not suffered, and I will show you one who has not lived.

This is a realization which I had to acknowledge long ago, but which has helped me walk with a strong gait, regardless of the load I was carrying. And by that I mean I had to accept my failings, limitations, and unmet desires as best I could. I had to look forward, to cast away all that would bind me, to forgive myself for my continual blunders, to humbly pray for guidance when necessary, and from then on it was only a matter of sticking to the grindstone, and learning to love this life which is worth loving.

*

17

five

Occasionally I was lucky enough to run into a kindred soul who was passing through Delhi for a short spell, and, upon meeting and becoming acquainted, we would enjoy each other's company for a few days, which allowed me the necessary respite of communion, before we inevitably said our goodbyes and I was yanked back into my solitary labors.

One fellow I met in a dirty little restaurant in the old city, was a long-haired Brit who had come to India for a number of reasons, one of which was to seek out a venerated astrologer living in the area. This Brit, Thomas, had read a few books by the astrologer, but had not considered visiting him until a month earlier, when, back in England, Thomas had the inspiration that he should go to India. Although he was penniless at the moment of his inspiration, circumstances worked in his favor- as they do when providence is at the wheel- providing him, within little more than a month, enough money to undertake the inspired journey, and there he was.

He and I spent a number of evenings together, sitting on the rooftop of the Camron Lodge, drinking rum, and discussing the subtle forces and subliminal fields which create the conditions of one's life and destiny. Thomas had a wise carelessness about him, which made him a pleasant companion, though this unconcerned disposition of his was largely due to the fact that he had fatalistically given himself over to impervious powers, which were in control of his life today and forever. It was this acceptance of his powerlessness which gave him such apparent equanimity and poise. However, one day he came to my hotel room a broken man. He had just come from seeing his astrological idol, who had read his charts, and failure was written all over Thomas' face.

Apparently the highly respected star-reader had told Thomas that he was on the completely wrong path, and that he should give up his metaphysical yearnings, return to England, go to a trade college, and learn some sort of useful workingman's occupation. Thomas was devastated. And not only that, he was in full confidence that this guru was correct.

I was in disbelief, although I can see now that Thomas's seemingly unshakable nonchalance and inner peace were merely phantoms easily extinguished the moment his idealistic beliefs turned against him. Which is to say that all was well and good with him when he was a seeker, a wanderer, and man of the spirit, but it all turned sour when he became a ditch-digger or an electrician, which were the types of fate that he now seemed reluctant and yet determined to accept.

18

Well, I gave it my best shot to convince him that this astrologer was a charlatan- as all 'experts' are charlatans, no matter what their faculty- and tried to persuade him that there was only one voice worthy of listening to- his own. I'm not certain how well I succeeded, however, because when a person has given their power away, and wants to give it away, there is little chance of helping them win it back.

Thomas and I parted a few days later, and off he went to whatever demoralized destiny he had finally accepted, and off I went to the one I had accepted.

A number of weeks later I was again granted a brief respite by the appearance of a middle-aged Australian vagabond named Arnold, who had been to India many times before, but had returned this spring not out of personal desire, but instead to search for his older brother, who had disappeared without a trace a number of months earlier. I was glad to have Arnold's company, but sad for him because of his almost certain loss. He and I spent a few days together, going around to travel agents, shopkeepers, and government offices, distributing his brother's photo and description, though we both had little hope that the search would turn out favorably. For the most part we simply hung out together, and found communion in that foreign land from which neither of us had any idea when we would leave.

Arnold was a brilliant talker, when his mind turned away from its sorrows. He was the type of guy who had read so much, thought so much, and conversed so much, that he was a neverending wellspring of fringe concepts, obtuse understandings, and esoteric tales. And it was a fabulous treat for me to be amongst a member of my tribe, and to sit back and listen to his assimilations, evocations, and conclusions about life and why it is the way it is.

And yet, of all the things about which he spoke during our days together, the stories of his brother were the most interesting to me, because, from Arnold's point of view, his brother was no less than a *mukta*- a God-knower. Albeit, his brother was a God-knower who had earned his daily bread by smuggling a half-kilo of hash out of India, rolled up in five gram balls, wrapped in cellophane, and swallowed into his stomach, every time he ran out of cash. But he was a God-knower nonetheless. And although I never met Arnold's brother, and cannot confirm his spiritual constitution, I can declare, from Arnold's descriptions of him, if nothing more, that I was hearing about one of a rare breed of individuals on this earth. Which is to say, I was hearing about ...a man. And by that I mean, I heard of an individual who lived without fear, without shame, without guilt, and without self-denial. And such descriptions in Arnold's stories about him kept me ever present in our lengthy conversations.

Half a year later I had returned to Canada, and had lost

19

Arnold's address, which was very disappointing to me because I not only enjoyed his company, and hoped to see him again someday, but I also wanted to find out if he was ever successful at uncovering clues as to his brother's whereabouts. Luckily the spirit runs thicker sometimes than others, and connections intended to be made are never lost. In this case, while I was in Canada, Arnold ran into my father, who was in India at the time, although they had never previously met nor seen pictures of each other. They happened to be in the same area, in a town in a northern Indian valley and Arnold "Just picked him out as a traveling Canadian"- as he wrote to me later- at which point he approached my father, and asked if he, my father, was who Arnold thought he was- and through their serendipitous, implausible meeting, Arnold and I were reconnected.

These types of magical non-coincidences happen, though generally for reasons beyond our ken, but to be sure, the universe is alive, and conscious, and fully aware of every grain of sand in the cosmic ocean of life.

One of those grains of sand also washed up on my barren shore in Delhi that winter, in the form of a beautiful and wise young Canadian woman, who to this day lives close to my heart, and close to the core of the Mother.[1]

I say such things because there is no better way to say them, though I do not in any way lay claim to understanding nor clarity, but when a person stands before me, and I can feel the core of their essence, and later have dreams regarding the nature of their being, then I make statements like I just did, for the only other option is silence, which may arguably be far more lucid and applicable than words, though still I cannot help but imperfectly groan about this miracle of life which is so far beyond me.

Anyway, before heading on to Darjeeling, which was where I had decided to flee when the chaos of Delhi had finally become unliveable, this aspect of the Mother, and I, had a couple of charming days together, sharing words and feelings, and basking in the spirit of Mother India, which culminated, the night before I left, with her and I sitting on the rooftop of the Camron Lodge, and witnessing the most ethereal, and beautiful pink dove go fluttering over our heads and then land on a nearby wire. To the materialist's mind it was simply a bird, but to the spirit eye it came as the holy ghost. And we received the descent of that heavenly gift, as the deep red sun sank beneath the Indian horizon. And in the morning I was gone.

*

---

[1] I sense that a woman is connected to the Mother- and by that I mean the Mother aspect of the Godhead- by the degree to which she is connected to the essence of her core, which is the Mother, for these two are not different; just as a man who lives from his center is one with the Father, as the saying goes.

six

In the Delhi train station that morning, in the frantic bustle while hunting for my carriage out of Delhi's tortured cosmolopolis, I had my day-bag and the back of my pants slashed by a malevolent urchin, who sought to rid me of my *rupees*, though fortunately all he got away with were a few condoms.

No matter, upon arriving in Darjeeling, two days later, I made my way to the small hotel which I had been directed to stay at by that brilliant young aspect of the Mother whom I had just departed from in Delhi. The hotel was located down one of the town's many dank and twisting, stone walkways, and after losing my way a number of times I finally ended up in the lap of one of India's most eccentric, incarnate expressions of the Mother- Amma Ongel, Mother Angel, owner of the Shamrock Hotel, a wayfarer's home away from home.

Amma was a rotund, fiery, loving and unbending matriarch. A woman who ruled her roost with care and an iron fist, making certain that each of her children- and anyone who arrived at her door was her child- were well-fed, well-bedded, and well-guarded from the insurrection of the night.

It was indeed a haven, a Shambhala for my soul, when I arrived into her bosom, and found myself eating home-cooked meals every night around a massive table, among other travelers, and being harbored from the neverending onslaught of invisible jackals at my heels. Amma received and released a multitude of souls like myself, all of whom came for corpulent sustenance acquired from the gravity of her soul's grounding. And when nourished they, like I, were sent off into the distance as if launched on the wings of her wisened dispassion. Roots and wings. Amma was the earth, but she did not withhold her children from the sky.

There were pictures in Amma's living room of her, this mother-to-all, standing with Nehru in the early 1950's, for her spirit had been a part of the birthing of Mother India, and she was resolute in her manner of approach, respect, and reproach, as necessary, to the entire populace of not only her country, but the entire world.

I was one of the many souls towards whom she had opened up her arms, had taken a liking to, and, after I had stayed with her for a while, she was even about to let me run the hotel for a few months while she was away overseas. That is, until she realized, in her own words, that I was "a drunkard and a womanizer"- facts which I could neither deny nor alter at the time. And who could blame me. I was

21

alone, and so I chose to booze. I was alone, and so I chased women.

I do not regret any of my absurd and societally unacceptable life back then. I accept all of myself, no matter who chooses to deny me. After all, I was no murderer or thief. All I wanted was some liquor and love. And who could blame me.

Regardless of Amma's outright decision, I did not hold it against her. She had to keep the cocks out of the henhouse, so to speak, and her decisions were based on the best for all. And so I continued to stay on at the Shamrock for a month or more, living in one of the lower, unheated rooms, during the month of January, when it is very cold in Darjeeling- so cold that I had to sit wrapped in blankets, attempting to warm myself with tea and rum, while hovering over the little kerosene stove I had purchased for 70 *rupees*, and then occasionally turning on my laptop, and continuing to pour out, from the neverending cauldron, the many ingredients lurking within me.

Anyway, as I said, I stayed on at the hotel for another month, and then headed south to find some warmth, if nothing more. A few months later I met up with Amma again, unexpectedly, in Bodhgaya, where I had been licking my metaphysical wounds while living in a small mud hut on a large property where many supplicants were engaged in a silent retreat, which is where I had decided was the next imperfect place to write, drink *chai*, become frozen in wonder, and go mad.

I ran into Amma on the street, and she was quick to convince me to help her put on a meal for about thirty Buddhist monks at one of the many monasteries in the town. And so I chopped vegetables one evening for her, and added my pitiful *baksheesh* into her limitless alms, and then we parted with a hug of love and understanding, going our separate ways. And so I left her like the prodigal son once again leaving the Mother's home, out again, away again, to spend and lose and gamble away all that I had been given, and all that I could not maintain, because I was like an insatiable man outside of the Garden, off of the conveyor belt, and I did not know that my pockets were empty, my vessel run dry, and my heart grown more barren on each exodus out and away and into the ungrounded cosmos, into the sky, where all spirits fly freely with wings but have no roots nor nest to which to return, and so they fly on and on, always imagining peace up ahead, always yearning to find and never finding what they left behind but did not know it- home.

I have seen men like myself running on that outer edge, along the precipice of non-being, balancing on the point of the furthest visible star in the galaxy, and hovering there, in the painful and yet untroubled distance, where only drink, or sleep, or madness brings relief from the inexorable need to keep running with abandon, always further out and away from humanity, society, rules, constructs, struggles, life, and love.

I too have walked through that void bounded by euphoria and despair, where the wings without roots fly effortlessly toward nowhere, because nowhere is the absence of all else, of all that befalls us in our tramp through the forest of futility and care.

I too have left this earth because it was not enough and far too much for me, and I too have found that once you break through the stratosphere of souls, it is almost impossible to get back, because to get back means to accept everything you have rejected in order to get away, and that reversal is a gross bathos from the untethered reaches back to earth, which is a turn-about that the free-flying spirit rarely, if ever, dares to choose.

However, as I often remarked to anyone who commented about how lucky I was to live so freely, to come and go as I chose, and to make decisions based on no one but myself and God- I often declared with absolute honesty that freedom means nothing without love, because without love, freedom is merely exile, for though it be the unchained spirit which lifts the wings to soar on high, it is the roots of love which give the eagle's wings its nest. For freedom without love is merely a massive prison without any rest, and nothing to do but fly on and on and on, because without love there is no home and without a home there is no such thing as freedom, only flight, because freedom is not love, but love *is* freedom.

*

seven

During my stay in Darjeeling, before heading south, I had run into a man named Hank, whom I had met only once previously, the night before leaving Canada for India, at a buddy's place who was holding a going-away party for me. Hank and I were both heading to the subcontinent within the next few days, and mutual friends at the party were trying to convince us to hook-up over there. Neither Hank nor I were moved by this idea however, for neither of us had an itinerary, a plan, nor a desire to have anything out in front of us fixed or related to time or calendars, for the spirit moves not to mankind's constructs, and neither Hank nor I worried about whether we would be guided to meet up, if such was the spirit's intention. And indeed, like two needles in a billion-stalk hay stack, we were magnetically drawn to each other on a street in Darjeeling, and have been good buddies ever since.

Things like this 'coincidental' meeting happen anywhere, and anytime, but for some reason such convergences seem to occur with greater frequency, and more improbability, in India, where the veil

23

between the whole and the parts is so transparent that at times it may as well not even exist; for the Mother is the matter into and from which all life comes and goes and finds its way without knowing why nor how. And it is only in a place like India, a land of a billion people, where a man can, for example, walk up to another man, in a random building in an bustling mountain village, and ask "Are you Jack Haas' father?", and there is a good chance the answer will be yes. It was the same with the meeting between Hank and I, for we were guided to come together, and the matrix of Mother India was the perfect living venue in which such subtle bonds like ours could come together in the chaos of the cosmic stew.

A similar occurrence happened on my first trip to India, when I had decided to include a brief visit to Nepal, so as to partake of the mountain culture, the Diwali Festival of Lights, and a glass or two of the rice beer called *chang* which I had heard so much about.

I left from Varanasi on a two day bus journey to Katmandu, and, as always, there were delays and unexpected breakdowns, and so, into the second afternoon it was obvious that we would not make our destination until very late in the evening. Although time had ceased to concern me at that point in my travels, I was admittedly anxious to get to Katmandu because, on top of the reasons mentioned above, I was also holding onto a thread of hope that I would meet up with a woman from Canada, whom I had fallen helplessly in love with during the previous year in Vancouver, although no tight bond had grown between us. And so I had left for India, and she for Thailand, and we had agreed to leave a message for the other person at a specific hotel in Katmandu, were either of us to get there on our separate journeys, so that we could attempt to meet up somewhere, if fate was to have it that way.

Well, to be sure, as providence always provides, I was on that tardy bus heaving its way over the broken dirt roads, winding through the mountains, and every once in a while the bus would stop in one of the sparse hamlets along the route, so as to take on more new passengers, all of whom were now forced to ride on the roof, as the bus was already crammed turgid with humanity inside. A few hours before arriving in Katmandu we stopped again, and I got off to release my bladder, and suddenly ran head long into the woman I adored, who a few hours earlier had gotten on top of the very bus I had been on for almost two days now, but I hadn't noticed because she had been sent up top. And so I had been riding along for the past many hours, anxious to know if I would ever see my heart's desire again, and she had been riding but a few feet above me all the while, and all you can do when the loving universe works such magic upon you is throw up your arms in bewildered hallelujahs, and ...make love.

Things like this happen, to be sure. A similar story comes from a very good friend of mine who was in India alone a few years

24

after that episode of mine, and she was on a bus heading through the plains when she got to talking to another westerner sitting in the seat beside her. It turned out, as they soon realized, that they were both from western Canada, had mutual acquaintances, and, in fact, were cousins who had never before met, though they knew of each other.

Oh, the ties are deep and unbreakable in the magic carpet woven by the invisible weaver who plays each thread into the unimaginable pattern desired at any specific place, at any specific time.

The spirit runs as thick as matter, and is matter, and all the separation and agony of the world are merely patterns in the living design, and the union and joy are but colors in those patterns which are not separated from the carpet, nor weaver, nor wearer, nor loom.

To continue though, having been guided to meet up with Hank in Darjeeling, I decided to join him and a few others on a ten-day reconnaissance trip into the Niora Gorge, a primitive valley in the lesser populated region of northern Bengal.

There were six of us who hiked into the valley from a nearby village, where we followed a river up to its source, and then traversed along a ridge at about three-thousand meters of elevation, walking on ancient yak trails, sleeping in bamboo shepherd's huts amidst gigantic rhododendron forests, and all the while being flabbergasted by the pristine beauty of one of India's last unlogged and unpeopled valleys.

It was a tremendous Himalayan adventure, not only because of the wilderness experience in the ancient land, but largely due to the presence and character of Hank himself, a big-bearded Canadian madman who, for the last fifteen years had spent six months every winter doing biological and ethnographic research in the mountains of India and Nepal. He had scoured the lands, journeying by foot, skis, bus, jeep, and elephant, to the most remote reaches of this timeless land, and had some fantastic tales to tell. For example: he claimed to have seen the stuffed remains of a small yeti, somewhere in a little mountain village in western Nepal, and then told how the mountain folk of Nepal know of hundreds of other 'little creatures'- the likes of which we call gnomes and goblins- and were as certain of these beings as they were of the sun.

Though it was not Hank's stories of other beings which were the most entertaining, but those which he related of himself. Like the time he was asked never to return to a certain Buddhist monastery after he was caught ogling a western woman's breasts, who was sitting near him during a 'closed-eye' meditation, at which point the lama became irate and declared that Hank was a pig from the fourth realm of hell.

Another time Hank spoke of beating up bandits who sought to rob him on one of the mountain routes which lay far into the hinter regions, but who failed because Hank was a towering, unbeatable force

25

of a man.

Hank had hundreds of personal yarns and anecdotes from his journeys throughout the mystic land, but one in particular springs to mind for its color and absurdity. Hank narrated how he and a buddy, who had joined him on an expedition into the rarely traveled areas of Uttar Pradesh, stumbled into a hidden cave where they were suddenly in the presence of a naked holy man who was sitting on the bare ground in the lotus position, with one hand held high in the air, and his penis tied in a knot around his massive beard. Note, I did not say his beard tied around his penis, and neither did Hank. It was a unique sight, to be sure, and one which might have caused anyone else on the planet to either kneel down in veneration to the yogi, or instead to leave quietly, out of respect for this sadhu who had most likely been sitting that way for years. Not Hank though. Oh no, he had seen every sort of mystery and inexplicable event known to mankind during his sojourns in the wondrous land, and so he did what he could not avoid doing- which is the one thing that, if ever he were to be called a saint, it would be for this- he burst out laughing. But it wasn't just a quick giggle at the absurd sight, and then on to more proper behavior. No way. Hank is as unbridled, unquenchable, and unabashed as they come. He was soon into uncontrollable howls, eventually falling to the ground in tears and laughter, and having to roll out of the cave and crawl out of the valley on all fours, as the hilarity possessed and weakened him like a child bursting with painful delight. Apparently his mirth was so contagious that his buddy was also on all fours with him, and unable to halt the stream of tears and hoots of unstoppable glee bursting through him. In fact, the two of them laughed for no less than two hours, at which point they were far away from the cave, where they slowly collected themselves.

Knowing Hank as I know him, and having been shown by him a great number of times that one of the essential ways of making it through the peril, stupidity, and pain of life, is to walk always with a light heart, I can bear witness *in absentia* to this happening, for Hank is the laughing saint who heals the world of its insanity and troubles with his lunacy and comic way. And though he is a very serious and caring man at times, he has trod upon this anguishing earth for so long, and seen such wonder and horror, that it seems somewhere along the way he walked out of the fires laughing, with sparks dancing in his eyes, and merriment cascading from his jowls, and for that I applaud and cherish him.

It is this foolish wisdom which I find so often sadly lacking within myself. The seriousness and outright weight of this life has often burdened me beyond what was necessary or healthy, so much so that at one time in my life, when I was deep into the muck and gore of existence, and could see no way out, my *anima* came to me in a dream, with the intent of showing me how to fly. In the dream she began floating upward, at which point she yelled out what I understood perfectly at the time- as one understands things perfectly in dreams- "Everything is light! Everything is light!" And I awoke knowing that the word 'light' is a *triple entendre*, and that the light which dissolves darkness is the same as the lightness which is not heavy, which is the same as the light-heartedness required to rise above the quagmire of struggle and concern. Indeed, I saw quite clearly then that the finished soul rises like a lotus out of the mire, and they rise out ...laughing.

And it was this same light- the light with three meanings- that I also knew would, if anything could, dissolve the manifold darkness within me which at times bored, oppressed, and blinded me to the privilege and delight of our blessed existence.

I was shown that the light-beings which we are, are only light enough to fly if we lighten up within. But to this day I have yet to find that essential lightness within myself, or any other, except in that whimsical, beautiful, and foolish wiseman- Hank, the laughing saint of the Himalayas.

Writing all of this down makes me wonder if in fact the world in which we live is already one designed for laughter and joy, and it is only my own misconceptions and false efforts that make it seem out of whack. And perhaps this is why twice in this lifetime God has come to me and unequivocally declared- "There is no problem!"

To be sure, I quickly rejoined that, from where I was standing, there were heaps of problems, though I can't argue with God, for when finally I entered unwittingly into God-consciousness, years later, during a shamanic journey on the discarnate wings of psychedelic mushrooms, there certainly were no problems, and, if there were ...they were hilarious.

There is no problem. The only problem is how to live without a problem. And that is a problem, for, at this point in the evolution of our species, humanity seems determined to cause its own grief, however obvious or obscure.

I have been coming to this notion for a while- that since most of our problems are self-created, true wisdom does not lie in solving problems, but in not causing them. Yet this type of *via negativa* is a truly subtle art, far too difficult for most base egos to sense or consider as an answer to the self-created conundrums and confusions which plague most lives. It is a true finesse, and one for which I claim no perfection- to live subtly, acceptingly, and consciously enough to cause ourselves, and therefore others, as little grief as possible- for though this may sound simple, it is perhaps the rarest of accomplishments in our strife-ridden world.

*

27

eight

Every morning on that trip into the Niora Gorge, just as the sun was coming up, Hank could be seen bolting frantically out of the hut for his morning bowel movement- an alarm clock for the rest of us which was as entertaining as his verbal diarrhea. Of course, over time, India inexorably creates such chaos in one's digestive track. In fact, on our hike out of the valley, after our ten day expedition was over, one of our team member's hemorrhoid's herniated, causing him to walk the rest of the way hobbling like a goose with a golden egg glowing red hot between his legs.

Such happenings are inevitable, however, while traveling about in the third world, where no one is immune from unavoidably developing some form of stomach upset, intestinal parasite, or amoebic dysentery every once in a while.

The two most memorable instances of internal upset I suffered while out and about in this marvelous, mischievous, maddening world, include one fine May day, when I was sitting on a beach in Gibraltar, after enjoying a hearty British repast which I washed down with a few pints of the Kingdom's finest ales, the likes of which I had longed for every day of my trip to Morocco, from where I had just returned, and where I had unknowingly ingested a healthy dose of some fairly tenacious vermin, which reared up its ugly head in grand, ignominious fashion, as I was sitting unwittingly upon that nice, British-clean beach, and leaned over to fart, and uncontrollably sprayed shit all over the back of my legs. Not a pleasant experience at any time, let alone on a beach dotted with translucent-skinned holiday-makers, none of whom were in the water, because it was May, and Gibraltar might as well be sitting in the North Sea at that time of year for the chill of the water temperature. No matter, I had to bolt from the back of the beach, through the labyrinth of prone bodies, and into the liquid-nitrogen, where I stood belly-button deep and humbly cleaned off my backside, to the curiosity of the crowd, after which I clenched my butt cheeks together, and waddled like a penguin back to my hotel room in Algeciras, Spain, where I spent the next four days spontaneously evacuating on the common throne.

It was an ego-reducing experience, to be sure, but still a mere slap on the backside compared to the kick in the crotch I received a few years later, during a forty-hour ride from Delhi to Kashmir, on a ramshackle old bus, full of angry Muslim men who were continually getting badgered by the Indian army at the omnipresent check-points we had to go through due to the armed uprising in the area.

28

In this second instance I had been toughing out a bad case of belly-ache and rectal discomfort as we lurched our way along the serpentine mountain highway towards Srinagar, on the last leg of our epic. A young Muslim fellow had befriended myself and a few other westerners, and was interpreting conversations between us and the driver. He was a good chap, whom at one point was curious to see my passport, which I handed to him. Soon after doing so I felt a surge of labor pains shoot from my stomach to my sphincter, and I knew I was about to give birth to a gruesome mudslide, on that bathroomless bus bound for a war-torn piece of heaven. I quickly asked the young Muslim fellow to beg the driver to pull over, which the driver refused to do, because the road was narrow and winding and we would be sitting ducks for other trucks coming along if we stopped. My entreaty had drawn the interest of the entire bus, most of whom seemed delighted at the thought of watching a spindly North American kid make a mess of his trousers. I had to use every ounce of strength I could muster to hold my rectum closed and stave off the breaking dam. And it was at the height of my anguish, when, perfectly choreographed, the young Muslim fellow, leafing through my passport, came to my photo and name, which caused him to hold it aloft, and, in great astonishment and glee, loudly announce- "His name is Jack Ass! His name is Jack Ass!" Which, as you can imagine, was impossible to deny at that moment.

I had my revenge, in a way, however, as I did not fill my pants on that bus, because, and only because, we came to another check-point within a few minutes after my alias had been unfortunately divulged. What happened is that I ran off the bus as soon as we were stopped, and made it quite apparent to the Indian soldiers what I was in need of, and was quickly directed to an outhouse about twenty meters away from the bus. After cathartically purging into the open pit below, I noticed that there was neither tap nor bucket of water on hand with which to wash my backside, as per the Indian way. Luckily I had a security package of toilet paper on me, and cleaned myself up the old western way, and left the outhouse. That was when the soldier, who was standing near the bus, looked towards me, knowing there was no water in the outhouse with which to wash my hands, and he made a 'want-to-wash-your-hands' signal to me, rubbing his hands together and motioning towards a nearby tap, to which I nonchalantly shook my head, and, to the disbelief of the officer, and, I hope, the whole spectating bus, I marched right back onto the bus, with what he and they must have assumed were shit covered hands. Take that you scoundrels. Make an ass of me and I'll do you one better.

I can't imagine what the other passengers thought of me, and it didn't matter, because the bus arrived in Srinagar soon after that, where I rented a wonderful houseboat run by a fantastic man. And the agony was over.

I sat alone later that night on the deck of that beautiful houseboat, on brilliant Lake Dal, in that mysterious land of Kashmir, soaked in wonder, and listening to the prayer songs of the old Muslim men come wafting over the water towards me from a mosque across the way. Rarely have I ever endured such a journey, and rarely have I endured such ecstasy and anguish at the experience of the unbelievable piety and sound coming upliftingly over the water to me; I was in ecstasy because I was there to hear it, and in anguish because no one was there to hear it with me. But that is life. You have to take the good with the bad or you get neither. If you want to eat, you've got to accept some shit.

And yet my best 'shit story' does not contain a momentous encounter with a fecal flood, but exactly the opposite. I'm speaking of the first ten days on of one of my trips to India- ten days in which I did not have a single bowel movement, which, to be sure, is a record on that continent of incontinence.

I had arrived in Madras as I always arrived on my extended overseas journeys- sick and lovesick. I had said goodbye to my lover of that time, had flown away indefinitely, and en route had been infested with a vicious bug during a two-hour stopover in Seoul, Korea, which caused me, by the time I arrived in Madras, to be in a feverish delirium.

I slept the first night on the cement floor of the Madras airport, and then took a rickshaw to a hotel in the city where I lay awake in agony for three days and nights, at the end of which I decided that if I was going to get better, it was not going to happen in such a barbaric metropolis, and so I made my way to the train station, bought a sleeper seat, and headed north towards my intended destination- the holy beach town of Puri, where I imagined a little sea breeze and a bit of ganja might ease the pain.

Upon arriving in Puri, a day or so later, I paid for a few days in a hotel, and then went to cash some traveler's checks at a nearby bank. That was when I found out that none of the banks in the area would cash Canadian traveler's checks. I was suddenly a very, very poor man, an untouchable, and had barely enough *rupees* left to buy a ticket for the next train to Calcutta- which wasn't leaving for another four days. And so I sat in that bed-bug ridden hotel room, ravaged both internally and externally by vermin I could not even see, aching from the love I had left forever across the other side of the ocean, and virtually penniless, existing on a few samosas per day. It was a good lesson, but one which would not come to fruition until I finally boarded the train headed slowly north, and it pulled into Calcutta, two days late, as per usual, and, in my delirium, I allowed myself to be misguided onto the wrong ferry across the Hooghly River, and then, soon after, I was caught in the slamming doors of a subway- which I had to take

30

since the ferry had left me nowhere near where I needed to be- because the doors I had been standing near would not open at my stop, and I was forced to charge through the crowded train to the next car, but then almost got carried away by the subway, because, although I was able to get through the doors before they closed, my backpack was caught on the inside, and no way to pull us apart, though I finally broke free in a feverish burst of violence. Then I wearily made my way to the hotel district where I was informed by the clerks at every front door that all the rooms were full, at which point I was broken and emaciated, and must have looked that way, because a young British trollop, who had been on the same train as I, took pity on me and offered to share her room, for which I was greatly thankful. But I still didn't have a *rupee* on me because the banks in Calcutta do not change traveler's checks either- you have to go to special 'money changers'- and with only a half an hour left before those closed for the evening I left my bag with the Brit and sped off, only to be misdirected a number of times again, until finally, with only a few minutes to spare, I arrived at the money changer's window and swapped a couple of traveler's checks for a few thousand *rupees*. I was saved. I may have been ill, famished, lost, loveless, and alone, but now I had money, and the sense of security it gave me allowed me to saunter serenely back toward the hotel, to stop for a victory soda at an outdoor stand, and then, at the moment I was thinking how safe I was, and how everything was going to be fine now that I had money again, I was smacked on the head by a massive wooden sign which came flying out of nowhere to strike me- one out of a billion people- and steal that assurance and calm out from under me with a near concussion. But that was all it took- ten days of sickness, poverty, despair, confusion, lostness, infestation, and now injury- that was all it took for me to learn what I was supposed to learn after ten days when I did not take a shit because I was either too ill or too poor to create the excess we have come to call shit- that was all it took for me to know that money cannot guarantee security, and the goose-egg left on my forehead after that was proof enough for me.

Oh, the spirit casts its gentle and not-so-gentle lessons down upon its cherished victims, and, to be sure, though most teachings are unpleasant, and, if not so, are humiliating, the ego and false understandings must be ever diminished, ever weakened, and ever broken in order for such simple wisdoms to penetrate our brutish craniums. Make that- *my* brutish cranium.

*

nine

There is a shift which occurs in life, a transition from the 'heading-out' stage, to the 'return' stage. I say that we begin the heading-out part of our separate journeys the moment we are born, as each of us sends ourselves out into the world of experience and challenge, building up a repertoire of acquaintances, characters, and other spirits which we meet along the way; and then we begin to 'return' when we stop venturing out into the world for learning and stimulus, and instead turn inward so as to process and debrief ourselves on what we found in the heading-out period. The latter stage is one of sorting and sifting through all the characters and experiences which we have assimilated into our souls during the former stage, bringing some of these aspects to the fore, while subordinating and rejecting others, as each of us attempts to find the perfect assortment and combination necessary to be whole, all the while slowly sailing back to the source of our origin, thus completing our life's journey.

I assume most people enter into the return phase around mid-life, which is why a crisis occurs for many at this time- because the soul is beginning to look the other way, towards home, and is tired of all the struggles and foreign adventures in the manifest. This shakes a person up who has come to identify themselves as the one who is heading-out, and who may have forgotten the place from whence they set off.

It seems to me that I turned around pretty early in life, at about twenty-seven years of age, for whatever reason I am not sure. I know that life in society and the goals it projects began to grow pale within me, and then went out completely, and all I was left with was a floundering ship, seemingly piloted by an invisible helmsman on an incredibly circuitous course home. I could say, in fact, that my whole life has been nothing but a journey home, only I had no idea where that might be, I merely knew that I had not found it amongst men.

In fact, trying to find a place in the world where I would belong was like trying to eat through my rectum, and shit through my mouth. And though the world had invented suppositories and emetics, these placebos led only to self-sodomy or ineffective purge.

When I ate of the world, I neither ingested, nor digested, I bled. I bled from the bosh and distractions of the day. My belly was full of society's poisons, and yet a great hunger still swallowed me whole.

The more the world disappointed me, or perhaps the more I disappointed the world, the more I retreated into myself. I sort of fell backwards for lack of trying to stand in the slight breeze.

People say that I became old too soon, that I surrendered too early, but that is the view of those accepting a world in which men tear each other to pieces for scraps. I simply stopped caring, and turned away.

By the time I was thirty years old and living in India, I felt like an eighty-five year old man, sitting on his porch, staring off to nowhere, having lost all aspirations to take part in the world.

I guess I fell away from it all too easily, lost my grip or something. What happened, I suppose, is that I could see how everything made by mankind was corruptible, that it was all in a state of chronic crumbling, and it was only through mankind's frantic efforts that things appeared to be well-ordered and in a state of homeostasis, but if you took away society's exhaustive labors for even a single day, the whole unsupported edifice would begin to tumble. And, as I saw it, nothing humans had produced was worth serving nor maintaining, and I was not willing to assist in the demented efforts to uplift and keep replacing the cards as they continued to fall from the house. I preferred to see it crumble. I preferred destruction. I preferred to see the orderly and yet intensely precarious structure fall into ruin, and see then what my fellow humans really were made of.

The shift, though, was an arduous one for me, as I slowly tacked and turned in the quiescent doldrums. At times I thought perhaps that I was missing something important- some vision, or passion, or trait which would have attached me to life and brought more excitement and vigor into my daily affairs. And yet, in a way, it was my distaste for the constructs of mankind that was itself the seed of a more integral, worldly interest. I say worldly, because with nothing created by mankind left to fall back upon, I was quickly alerted to the only things that remained- the earth, and the heavens. And so, in the act of distilling out the dross from the ore, so to speak, I was left with naught but the ingredients necessary to complete the alchemical stew: The earth, the heavens, and …me.

As such, during the shift, I instinctively fell into a moratorium from all concept and care. I lived on no truths for a time, mentally starving the world out of me; I fasted from 'what is', and was nourished on the wholesome fat of ignorance. I devoured the hunger in me, hungering without respite, until that hunger gnawed itself away. I was not satisfied, but I no longer hungered, for I had disentangled the heart from its losses, the mind from its news, and had unwound my somebodiness into no one.

Oh, many times after the shift began I longed again for life, for even a false meaning to return me to the tangible confusion I left for the intangible confusion I now could not leave; how I wished again to taste the world. But I was already gone. I did not stay. I left that place, unfollowing the path without direction, for I had said goodbye, and turned and walked away from everything. Everything. And when I looked back, searching for the 'me' that I had been, there was nothing left except a life that was no longer mine, passing away before my

33

eyes; I was drowning in mystery. I had looked too far, and finally had no image of myself nor of being.

It was a bizarre, unthinkable, disturbing place that I had gotten to, but I didn't go back, for I realized quickly that the only thing I longingly gravitated toward was the innocent wondering of our unknowable Creator; to sit and stare at nothing and infinity, that was all I wanted. The freedom to slow down, to stop, to exalt; I loved life too much to be busy.

And so I realized that loneliness was the only power I had over the world, and to be lost was the closest thing I could find to freedom, for everything else was a trap, because in the end, there was no solution except to tough it out. To sit with it, to feel it, to accept it, and to throw up my arms once again in agony, resignation, and hallelujah.

It was only in such ghostly solitude, only when I was alone, only when I was lonely, conceptually lonely, that I could dispute the dubious finitude that was myself. It was there, as the mystery engulfed itself in a breathless utopia of intimate strangeness that the tickling communion of grace would trickle down through my innocent nothingness. The methodology was easy- I simply forgot what I was told to remember.

And this ...this was the death I came to die. For truly it is a death to lose all need for the world; to do nothing, to think nothing, to be nothing. Yet a single moment of honest apathy is worth a thousand years of reckless striving.

Thus, as if the verdant and bloody field of Kurukshetra itself were laid out beneath me, I fought the world without fighting and did battle without battling, simply by holding firmly onto apathy- my aegis ...my shield against the tolerable. Which is to say: a miraculous privilege happened to me one day- boredom; I had tasted life, and found it bitter.

And so I came eventually to the point where I had narrowed my focus away from the world; I had closed my eyes and yet kept moving until the only thing I could sense was myself stumbling blindly. And though all around me was a boisterous crowd, excited and chattering, and heading the other way, I did not run to view what caused exuberance in the masses. *I kept on going towards where I happily ...had no idea.*

I did not so much as even look in the direction of the bold, glorious norm, but struck out instead within myself, and haunted down lost passageways, makeshift as if all my own. As if to solemnly stare through infinity, onto this glazed incongruous known, was now mine, and mine alone.

I neither acquiesced, nor adhered to the fake conclusions driven hard upon us all by the godless hordes about. I was in the war,

34

but I was no warrior, only an indifferent soldier gone AWOL in the glorious night; I was fugitive from both sides of the fight, caught in the soul's no-man's land, like a sacrifice the spoiled Gods refused to take.

And yet I still took part in everything. I went everywhere, thought every thought, loved every love, and suffered every pain, like all the rest, but none of it was mine- I did not belong and that is why I belonged. So you see where I was at then.

It was a strange concoction of merriment and writhing, in which the joy of life made the hurt that much more painful. The more I fled the thorns, the more I got pricked. The more I tried to grab the roses, the more I got pricked. The thicket grew around and through me. The more I ate, the more I breathed, the more I thought, hoped, attempted, or cursed, the more I got pricked. Still I fought hard against the crime of our earthly destinies.

At one point in my life, while I was back in North America, and experiencing a similar estrangement from all that is, I was compelled to head out one cold and miserable February day from Vancouver, towards my haven on the coast- Flores Island. It took me two full days of hitchhiking and bussing to finally make it to the little hamlet of Tofino where I caught a Native-operated water-taxi out to the island. Upon arriving, just as the sun was going down, I began a two-hour hike to the far, wave-beaten west coast, and the destination of my pilgrimage.

I remember the darkness and mist falling upon me as I slogged onward and entered the last part of the trail leading to a secluded beach where few others ever came, and so it remained a natural bastion of isolation and purity. And I remember that only a few hundred metres into the bush my flashlight went dead. And I remember at first stumbling about trying to refind the trail, and not being able to find it, and then spinning around thinking I could hear the ocean, and following the sound, then realizing it was only the wind in the trees, which meant I had been flailing in an unknown direction, and then I began stumbling through marsh and swamp, and climbing over endless deadfall and through ferns and salal, and imagining what a torturous night it was going to be in this wet and freezing west-coast jungle. And I remember finally coming to a stand-still from lostness and exhaustion, and leaning against a great tree, and looking up to the heavens, and uttering the words I suppose I was meant to utter from the outset of my journey- "OK, OK, you've got me now." And I gave up. And I remember how in the moment of that acceptance and surrender I was as if wiped clean, as if the prodigal part of me had been returned again to the home of my beginnings, and I was reunited with the source again, and suddenly without thinking or questioning, or wondering about direction or distance, I started off going again, with a newfound determination through the undergrowth, for I had returned to the spirit by giving up the ghost. And I remember finally making it through to the edge of the forest, and stepping out onto a darkened beach, and realizing that I had come out just a few feet away from where I had intended to end up, and despite my frantic confusion I had been guided through it all along, and all I had needed to do was surrender and allow it to be so. And I remember the cheers of gratitude and relief that leapt out of my mouth right then, flying off into the empty night for no one to hear but the trees, the ocean, my God and me.

And then I remember arising early the next morning, and feeling that I had still some fight and unpeace left within me, and in the damp and bite of the west-coast winter I set off down the massive beach, as I had done in this very place so many times before, walking up and down to beat the taint and thickness out of me. And somewhere along the middle of the day I remember turning to face the ocean, and in the empty, capitulative openness which comes from such solipsistic mortifications, throwing up my arms and asking why I had needed to come all the way out here, again, why had I to face the loneliness and discomfort again, why I had been told- "Get ye to the sea my son", again. And I remember how obvious and easily the answer wafted through my mind; a simple answer, one that a child could have told me, but an answer I would not have understood until I had been whipped and frozen by the world, had lain down and been lifted up and lain down again because I could not do what I was supposed to do, which was the answer to my lostness all along, and the answer was- "Just Be!"

And as I fell softly into the rhythm of myself once again, and calmly began to walk along the beach, I realized my lesson was over. And I strolled back to camp, packed up my belongings, and prepared to venture forth again into the world of men from which I had just been driven, only a day earlier, but now I came back to share the commandment which had been spoken to me from the sky- "Just *Be!*"

For there is no moment, no event, no grain of sand, no laughter, no death or healing, no thought or feeling, no tear or yearning out of place. The cosmos is eternally complete. There is no problem if only we would just be. That is all that is asked of us. As simple, and difficult, as that.

*

ten

Prior to the shift of which I have just spoken, life was not such an overbearing weight pressing down upon my furtive countenance, nor hounding me day in and day out. Oh no, I had my day of revelry and laughter, to be sure. And by that I mean I had many years of ribaldry, tomfoolery, pranksterism, and otherwise attempting to cause others as much brotherly grief as possible. And when the final accounts are taken, those years of uproarious delinquency might actually balance out against the debits of melancholy with enough credits of fatuity that my ledger will be clean.

Much jocularity existed in my life during my early years, and reached a sustained crescendo while I was in university, for by then academia had turned sour for me, and I had become painfully bored of the whole mess, and then downright contemptuous, which is why I turned swiftly away from those hackneyed ways and took up my higher calling of beer swilling, partying, and causing as much catastrophic turmoil to my mates as I could muster.

In a way I must have already made the decision *against* studies, and *for* carousing, on the first day of frosh week, because upon arriving in the massive co-ed dorm in which I was to live out my first year of university, I was asked by one of the floor supervisors to assist a few other freshmen to move a large number of cases of beer from the lockup into a common room where soon the inaugural festivities were to begin. And so I trundled up many flights of stairs with the others, and into the lockup, and when we came out- each of us toting forty-eight bottles of beer- the rest of the crew turned right, and I turned left, and ran right back down those same flights of stairs and into my dorm room, and suddenly I was a couple of cases of beer to the good, which, combined with the two forty-ounce bottles of Jamaican 151 proof rum I had brought in my suitcase, made for a fair beginning to the wild and wonderful frosh week about to begin. The mayhem had started.

Soon enough I was linked to a gang of jokers and jackals, and if we weren't scaling the outside of buildings in drunken bravado, we'd be hiding on one of the upper balconies, and showering cabbies and cops with a sortie of eggs. And if that turned monotonous we'd be covering people's rooms in shaving cream, maple syrup, or wet flour.

Or perhaps we'd forsake the unrelenting desire to cause material grief, and would instead enter upon some well thought-out psychological damage, like sneaking into a person's dorm room in the middle of the night, then slowly placing an obnoxious sounding music tape into their stereo cassette, cranking the volume to full, and then getting out of the room before the silent leader on the tape had ended and the apocalypse begun.

It was astonishing, after such an event, if one of our hapless victims came bursting out of their room in a fit of anguish or rage, to see how bone-white their flesh had become, after being awakened unexpectedly in such traumatic fashion.

Unfortunately most of the victims caught on quickly and

would be sure to lock their doors at night, a factor which we soon got around, however, by hiding wind-up alarm clocks in remote areas of their rooms, sometimes in the deepest recesses of the hanging ceilings, while the luckless sots were being distracted out of their rooms, during the day, by a comrade.

I would lie in my own bed later that night fighting off the giggles while thinking of the alarm firing off at 3:00 am, and the ensuing search and accompanying agony and fury involved. It was no less than pure joy to bring such catastrophic novelties into another's life. Pure joy.

The next year I moved into a nine-bedroom house, which left the other poor occupants as sitting ducks, for now even locked front doors could not keep me and my accomplices out, for the villainy lived within. This caused the inhabitants to suffer ongoing calamities such as having their toothpaste tube injected with Preparation H, which, if you know anything about that hemorrhoid ointment, has quite a severe burning effect when spread upon soft tissue.

And if that wasn't enough, and it wasn't, I was in the habit of carrying around with me a small tube of oral novocain gel, which came out of the tube clear, and therefore could be squeezed inconspicuously amongst the bristles of an unguarded toothbrush, without the owner noticing- not, that is, until they had finished brushing their teeth and the entire inside of their mouth had been frozen numb- a startling and inexplicable occurrence which caused no little amount of hypochondria and worry.

No one was safe nor immune from such antics, and though I certainly received my fare share of retribution from the victims, the assaults upon my well-being simply spurred me on further.

As such, one night my pernicious comrades and I completely outdid ourselves.

It happened one evening, during my second year of institutional torture, when four of us were living in the basement quarters of that big nine-bedroom house.

A buddy and I snuck stealthily on all fours into one of the lower bedrooms occupied by a woman friend of ours, while she was asleep in bed. But this time not only did we set the alarm to go off in the middle of the night; we also set the clock forward, so that when it rang the clock would read 7:30 am. Time to get up.

Furthermore we hung a light-bulb outside of the house, near her window, to simulate morning, and a few hardy, determined cretans and I stayed up until 3:00 am, sitting in our night-clothes, in the downstairs kitchen, and eating cereal, so that when her alarm went off, and she thought it was 7:30 in the morning, she got up, had breakfast with us, did her hair, made her lunch, and left for school soon afterward.

Boy did we pay for that one, though it didn't deter us, not even slightly. As much psychological confusion and damage as we could mete out without doing personal injury- that was our unwritten *modus operandi.*

Another strategic assault upon an individual's peace and self-confidence came in a few bold maneuvers against a wiry, young Bermudian fellow who had come to Canada for his university education and who was rooming with one of my mates at the time. This bloke returned to Bermuda every Christmas, spring-break, and summer holiday, and he once told us that everyone who entered Bermuda, be they citizens or visitors, was subjected to a thorough search of their luggage, as the authorities were painstakingly neurotic about drug smuggling.

One night before he flew home, this fellow had passed out from an excess of drink, which allowed us to sneak the filthiest, most horrific, triple-x pornographic magazine we could find into his suitcase, of which he knew nothing, until he was standing in the Bermuda airport, with a brutal hangover, in front of the customs officer going through his bags, and suddenly she had the periodical in hand and was holding it up in somber scrutiny, at which point the poor wretch became mute with disbelief.

That was a good one, but we weren't through with him yet. He was still smiling too much. Thus I took it upon myself to enter his bedroom whenever I was over visiting my buddy, who was his roommate, and the unfortunate lad was out, the intent of which was to turn his waterbed heater up to full blast, which, if you know anything about water, heat, and convection, would cause the temperature to rise slowly, but then become a steaming cauldron which would not cool down for days after the mischief had been discovered. Often he was pissed at me for a few hours when he discovered that his pancreas was overheating, but he soon got over it and all was forgotten. That is, until the time his roommate and I installed an extra, hidden heater under his water mattress, and ran the electric cord out the back corner, and into an unused plug, and then turned both heaters on full blast. And my God did we howl.

About a week later the Bermudian lad was in a fit of rage, claiming that I must have broken his waterbed heater because he had discovered that it had been turned up, again, a few days earlier, and although he had turned it down, the water was still a boiling vat, upon which he was writhing in sweat and discomfort every night.

Well, in the practiced, matter-of-fact presence which I had come to embody at times requiring such histrionics, I simply denied having broken his heater, which was true, and dismissed his charges as pure libel.

Three weeks later my partner in crime and I entered the abject fellow's room when he was out, and found the heater we had surreptitiously installed under his bed now severed from its wiring harness, as if our victim must have finally stumbled upon it, and in a fit of deranged mania torn it in half, a feat requiring no small amount of determination nor strength, and one which, upon observing the outcome of our games, left us in uncontrollable eruptions of hysterics and cackles, the magnitude of which may have even given Hank, the laughing saint, respect for our zealous and passionate undertakings.

*

eleven

Back in India, a number of years after my ill-fated trip to Puri and Calcutta, which ended in the massive sign descending onto my cranium, I was to meet up again with the same force which had chastened and bludgeoned back then, though in this new encounter I was not to receive a heavy-handed lesson, but instead a blessed gift.

I was on my way down from the Ladakhi plateau, where I had been traveling with my *soror*[2], my mate of a number of years by this point, on this most recent of my visits to the subcontinent.

We were headed back to Delhi, after spending two months together in the high-altitude northern states of Spiti, Lahaul, and Ladakh, including a two-week stay in the state's capital, Leh.

In Leh we had found ourselves in the presence of a Buddha, who was well disguised in the being, personage, and character of the owner of a family-run hotel which we stayed in, on the outskirts of the town. This fellow had never been outside of Ladakh proper, except for a short trip to the city of Jammu. Other than that he had remained in this one area his whole life, and yet he was not only as worldly as any traveler who had spent their whole life on the road, but he also cast forth an otherworldly smile like I had never seen before, nor since. Good God could that man smile. And it was not a smile belonging to the demure, enchanting, Sophia-like grin of the Mona Lisa, but an all-out, ear-to-ear, I-can't-believe-how-great-it-is-to-be-alive, childish, spontaneous, unabashed, tremendous, uplifting smile. That man smiled a smile I had never seen on another person. And I had certainly seen Tibetans, Nepali, and Sherpas smile, and nobody on earth smiles like these folks, as if no other culture has tapped as deeply into the

---

[2] The *soror mystica*, or mystical sister, is the female of the male-female partnership seeking the alchemical gold of life.

40

bottomless wellspring of joy hidden but not obstructed by the troubles of the day. In my time amongst those folks I had seen smiles that made me insane with disbelief, because they arose instantly, for only the slightest of reasons, and cast the rapture of existence out at me and wham!, one moment I was face to face with one of those hard-working, somber-seeming mountain folk, and then, in the twinkling of an eye, I was standing in the presence of Bodhidharma himself, whose joyous wisdom now radiated uninterruptedly out of his eyes, jowls, lips, and cheeks, destroying not only me but all agony in that smile's path. Those mountain people can surely smile. Compared to them no one in the western world has ever even smirked, except perhaps the laughing saint, who must have received his mirth osmotically, from so many years in that psychic atmosphere. And yet, all of those delirious, unstoppable, unquenchable, uncanny smiles I had witnessed in my Nepali friends and Tibetan acquaintances over the years were but mere grins of amusement compared to the smiling, unflappable cheer that radiated at me through the face of this humble husband, father, gardener, hotel-owning, bidi-smoking Buddha who killed me with his joy.

That man was a gift, to be sure, but a blessing of a different kind was about to follow, as our stay with him had finally ended, and now my *soror* and I were on a bus headed south, after which she was to fly back to Canada, and I was to stay on for another ten days in Delhi and continue to write. I was in the midst of a book I had been working on for quite a while, and was in a fever to finish it because I had lost my love-affair with words at the time and was therefore pressed into the uncomfortable position of having to complete what I had begun- a task which I met with the determination and delirium of a runner who knows not when the race which has exhausted him will ever finish.

Luckily the spirit was strong with me, as they say, and must have been feeling a bit of sympathy for my labors, on that journey down from the purified heights to the lowlands, because, although I had relinquished smoking any form of cannabis at that point, our bus was heading through the hash-haven of the Himalayas, the Kullu Valley, where we were planning to stop for a few days and get a room in Vashist before continuing on to Delhi, and I was feeling free from such abstemious mortifications. So I let myself consider revisiting Shiva's cerebral sanctuary as an open possibility, largely because I was seriously worrying that ten days in the tortured metropolis of Delhi was going to be an endurance test for me, as the last time I had been there, writing for months on end, I had escaped barely intact from that punishing, cataleptic wrestling match with the stubborn muses. And so I got to thinking that a little bit of hash might make my stay a little more comfortable. And yet I decided that I would not actually buy any hash, but instead would scour my hotel room, and if I found any chunks

41

or pieces dropped by stoned travelers in the past, I would take this as a blessing, and consider it God's gift to allow me little mental holidays over the next week and a half, so as to survive Delhi during my studious endeavors.

Well, as odds had it, I did find a nice little chunk- about half a gram- of the black gold, which was smeared into the jute mat covering the floor of our room, and I took this as the go-ahead from the spirit. The little nugget was no ingot sized monolith, by any means, but plenty enough to trigger my purified insides into the necessary reactions.

After arriving in Delhi a few days later, my *soror* jumped on a plane, and I booked into a hole-in-the-wall hotel room, in the old part of the city, for the next ten days of writing, reading, typing, editing, and, when each day was finally over, of having a puff of the blessed resin and letting the mind wander away from its prison.

All things come to us, be they good or bad, if we either need or deserve them, for the mirror of the external is always perfectly polished and ever-ready to spontaneously reflect back our internal lives, in manifold ways, so as to symbolically applaud the spirit's intent within the show.

In this case, about five days into my daily labors and evening flights, I was out for a meal and fell to chatting with an Indian Sanskrit scholar and poet, whose name, interestingly enough, was Ashish Dube, which immediately made me think of hashish doobies. Very odd indeed, because I was smoking the hashish I had considered a gift from the spirit, and this was now mirrored perfectly in my acquaintance's name, a name which was not only phonetically similar to my manna, but which in Hindi means: blessing.

All is reflected through all. All is all. We may think this is a piecemeal creation, but to be sure, it is as contiguous as the sky. All things shift and pull, in tune and time with our lives, and all events harbor a greater intention.

It is for this reason that at times I accepted circumstance, allowed that the greater will would administer existence better without my interference, and so I gave back what was not really mine anyways, by relinquishing the knowledge of what I could no longer pretend to understand. At times I chose to be blind and stumbling and guided by another, larger vision, than to continue being directed by my own finite sight.

To be sure, in lesser dimensions I could have easily contained a juvenile longing requiring no such sustained appeasement of being's infinitude, but in higher dimensions I confronted a bewildering apparentness that allowed for no assuaging stimulus, whether harbored or relinquished, simply because I was now obliviously aloft amongst the ubiquitous mystery and its neverending suddenness, and therefore dependent on nothing and interdependent on everything.

For there is nothing on the outside that is not on the inside also. And in the end there are not two worlds clashing at the membrane of the self, but only two aspects of a singular happening, which ebb and flood into each other. And it is we who construct the locks and canals between the two, inhibiting the flow between them, for the finite ego lives at the estuary, while the infinity of God lives at the source.

And so I say that because the God force within us is the same as the God force without, when we harmonize with that singular source, all surrender and rebellion are the same act, and at that point, no matter what goes on, life *is* divine intervention, though it becomes more apparent when we tune our radios to that hidden song.

And yet all those who do blend in and become one with the greater rhythm still know nothing of its meaning, message, nor means, but only that it cannot be heard with the ears, nor described by the mind, but only felt and followed by spirit joined to the heart levered open.

It's all in the rhythm. It's all in the eternal dance dancing to the eternal rhythm in the glory field stretched out ponderously over the soporific veil. It's the rhythm of stillness and pandemonium, harmonizing in the rapture of now. It's when meaning and need shatter into the wantless glow flowing through the static poverty. It is the crush and bend and the unbroken laughter married to the neverending sigh. It is a rapture and a longing danced in the sorrow-soaked ecstasy of life's abandon.

I have danced in that dream where the pentecost and penance rise alongside each other, as two helixes bound in a single strand of awe. As if I came to this realm of flesh for naught but to swim dancing in a medium of love, anger, spirit, pus, urine, milk, flesh, and blood. As if I was born into the entrails of a dying beast, and only in its death did I come to life. As if God's hyenas tore into the carcass of this realm, and as their jaws came crashing through their game, I was set free from death, decay, and all that spoils the cosmic brew. As if to that death which birthed me I now turn back towards, like an astronaut leaving his own solar system for another. I see where I have been, but not where I am going. I know only that through the death from which I was birthed, I learned how to crawl, to walk, to run, and then ...how to fly.

*

twelve

All is reflected through all. All is all. These may seem like trite platitudes shot out of an inaccurate weapon at a target so big it cannot be missed, but axioms like these are displayed time and again in the minutiae of the manifest.

I'm thinking, for example, of my time spent dwelling in another room of the Mother's house- the Mother Earth- a year or so after that last sojourn to India. I was camping near the windswept, black-sand beach in the utopic Waipio Valley, on the northeast side of the Big Island of Hawaii. I had hitchhiked with my *soror* from Hilo, up island, to the rim of the Waipio Valley, from where we walked down the precipitous, four-wheel-drive road which leads to the bottom of the vale. There we forded a river, and made our way onto the east-facing, marvelous stretch of black sand, dotted in behind by a sparse forest of ironwood trees.

In looking for an appropriate place to set up our tent, we happened upon an oddly primitive and yet well maintained 8ft×8ft hut, built completely of bamboo. It was seemingly abandoned, and so we set up our tent beneath the awning, and stayed there for the next few days, occasionally gathering avocados, citrus fruits, and macadamia nuts, which we roasted in the hollows of rocks placed in a fire. There was a pure spring bubbling up in a nearby property, from which we gathered drinking water, and so the whole scene began to take on a paradise-like quality, the likes of which only such Caucasians as Robinson Crusoe, or Gilligan had ever before experienced.

After a few days in the valley together, my *soror* had to return to Canada, but I stayed on, camped beneath that bamboo wonder, nibbling upon the fruit of the land, walking the lengthy beach, and reading G.K. Chesterton's biography of St. Francis of Assisi, which I had purchased for a few sheckels earlier at a local market.

I was impressed by St. Francis, that gentle titan who one day simply up and quit the world, but didn't leave. Not Francis, not that unobtrusive zealot. He could have wandered off into the forest alone, and stayed there, and had a merry old time of it basking in the warm and sustaining glow of the spirit, far out and forever beyond the turmoil of the day, but he didn't. Francis stripped himself bare, declared he neither needed nor wanted a single thing from mankind, and then proceeded to live amongst the faithless throng, like a self-enclosed beast, neither needing clothing, nor shelter, nor money, but only Christ and the earth to sustain him. "My brother the wind, my sister the rain", declared Francis, one who had crossed the invisible threshold into the realm of peace and union, and yet remained among all men divided from the source.

St. Francis belonged to both God the Father and also God the Mother- to the spirit and to the earth- which is why he, like Christ, also fled to the solitudes of the Mother, the earth, for his communion with the Father, before returning to a world which was doing its best to belong to neither.

44

I spent the next few days hanging about in that pacific paradise while polishing off the book. Occasionally locals would pass by for a chat, some of whom made mention of the hut I was staying in, although there seemed to be a fair bit of confusion as to the name of the character who had built it. And it was not until I left the area, climbed back out of the valley, stuck my thumb out for a ride, and was picked up by a woman who lived in the region that I found out the truth. She told me that the man who built the austere hut had once been a high salaried professional in some technological field or other, and then one day, for reasons known only to himself and God, he quit his job, renounced everything, entered the Waipio valley with nothing but a machete and some matches, changed his name to Ken, built his little hut, made clothing out of coconut hair, learned to live off of what Mother Earth provided, and invited anyone faithful or brave enough to come and join him at the place he now called 'Homecoming'. In short, he had pulled off the St. Francis gambit, had walked away from the corruption of mankind, and back to God and the earth, thus bridging the gulf between the spirit and matter, just as his predecessor had done.

It was no great surprise, then, that I had been reading Francis' biography, while unknowingly staying in a hut built by one of his own, or perhaps even an incarnation of that old druid himself, St. Ken of Waipio.

Individuals such as Ken, St. Francis, and Christ, have somehow found within themselves the endurance, tenacity, and passion to live both upon this earth and within the heavens. To live in one of these is enough for most of us, and few, in fact, live in either; most of us exist at the intertidal zone, where neither a house nor a garden is possible due to the flood, nor an ark nor a fishing-line for the ebb. And so we do not really exist at all, because we belong neither to the heavens nor the earth, and are as if fleshless phantoms, or spiritless bodies, aimlessly wafting about without mooring, and blowing about without wings, and wondering why life is so meaningless, so agonizing, so odd. And the answer is because we do not exist- not until we take up our citizenship in the heavens, or build our love upon the earth.

To find our homes in either of these realms would lodge us finally into a life where we might find peace, and beauty, and worth, but then to look upon the likes of Francis, and Christ, and know that they somehow set both their roots on earth, and their wings in heaven, is to understand the distance we still must go in order to be whole.

To walk that diaphanous bridge- wherein the spirit descends into matter, and where matter rises to spirit, and in that union a new quality is born, a new frequency is found, and the cosmic radiations infuse the earth energies with their intimacy, the Mater becomes the Pater, and the pattern enters the matter- to walk that diaphanous bridge is to marry once again the two realms to which our beings belong, and which are united in, and of, and through us.

*

thirteen

I am no Ken, and no St. Francis, have never thought I was, nor tried to be, and am not drawn to- or perhaps am repulsed by- the idea of absolute renunciation. I have mortified and denied myself improperly enough in this lifetime to know that such asceticisms require no small amount of dexterous mastery, which only too easily goes wrong, and therefore I shy away from them, like a child away from fires by which he has previously been scorched. I do, however, believe in our need to live on and with the earth, as well as in and of the heavens.

In fact, the next time I was on the Big Island of Hawaii, I took the opportunity to build a primitive hut of my own. Though it was not at all primitive compared to Ken's, as I used three felled Ohia trees for the frame, a large industrial tarp for the roof and water-catchment system, and about forty feet of greenhouse shade-cloth for the walls, so as to keep the bugs out but allow the ever-blowing Hawaiian breeze in.

When building that little hut I was intending to construct it in such a way that everything was level, firmly rooted in proper joints and bracings, and otherwise fit to fulfil an engineer's specifications. However, although I had learned some mortise and tenon joinery, some cabin building techniques, and a bit of masonry in the past, I soon realized that the only skills I was employing in the creation of my hut were ones I had learned while at play building forts during the summers of my youth, in the forest behind my Grandmother's cottage in upstate New York. I also realized that it was only in my 'adult' life that I had been corrupted by the idea of perfect angles, sheer strength, and building codes, none of which mattered here, nor, I hope, will ever matter, for though I plan someday to construct a more substantial abode for myself, somewhere on this marvellous earth, I vow within myself to use as little modern technology and practicality as I can, and instead of building a home, I vow to build a fort.

Anyway, it took me only a day or so to create a liveable Tarzan's hideaway, in which I took up residence for nearly two months, near a Hawaiian holy site, with views of both Mauna Kea and Mauna Loa, and surrounded on all sides by wild bamboo orchids and a few mango trees. The hut was on a parcel of land which my father, brother and I had planned to purchase together, as land was incredibly cheap on

46

the south-east side of the Big Island, due to Pele's[3] unpredictable landscaping impulses. Unfortunately the deal fell through because the bluffer who owned it reneged at the last moment- like all bluffers, who say one thing but do another and are so full of excuses and explanations employed so as to sanitize their inability to keep their word- and I was left to walk away from my prized hut, my fort, and wander out and away again, into the crazy, fabulous, implausible world.

But before that all happened I lived in the hut, on the earth, for over two months, and because of my newfound connection with the earth's energies, I was, without intention, bridging the very gap which divides us all inwardly, and so divides the earth and heavens outwardly.

I say this for a number of reasons. Firstly, because during those two months I was almost completely alone, and yet so grounded by the earth that I must have been capable, at that time, of receiving a visitation by a force which would have incinerated me had I been unattached to anything capable of buffering the charge. I am speaking, of course, of God, who came to me in a dream one night, wherein I was suddenly speaking to a being wearing an amorphous mask, which, after a while, he, or she- for the person was quite androgynous- took off the mask, and, lo and behold, it was God explaining to me that he, or she does not show his, or her face to many people, because, it seemed, he, or she was saying, no one was all that interested anymore. Well, to be sure, I was interested.

This may all sound like a bit of crack-pot stage theatrics, but on the day after the dream, or visitation, as you will, I had resumed reading a spiritual book which I had started a week or so earlier, and it all of the sudden made reference to Joseph Campbell's book series, *The Masks of God*, which was a synchronicity that further validated my experience.

Campbell would make another literary appearance in my life a few weeks later, after a night in which I had experienced a most lucid and convincing event I can only describe as 'moon consciousness'. This came about as I was sitting under a full moon, and sensing without a doubt that I was within the moon's consciousness- that She was cascading Her consciousness down upon me, upon the land, and upon all others under the light of the night. It was a very strange reckoning, a very compelling connection, and a very telling episode which made me understand why civilization, specifically city culture, is as crazed and out of balance as it is: there is no moon consciousness in the city, because the electric lights completely obliterate not only Luna's visual amplitude, but also her psychic effect on humanity, and therefore those in the city live only under sun consciousness, which becomes oppressive and despotic when not balanced out by the moon.

---

[3] Pele is the Goddess in Hawaii, and She *is* the volcanic activity.

47

Soon after that experience I was to once again come upon a book, this one by Joseph Campbell himself, titled *Transformation of Myth Through Time*, and I had it in my hand for only a few minutes before I skimmed ahead and landed on a chapter in which an alchemical drawing, originally brought to attention by W.B. Yeats, showed an altogether unknown 'cycle' of the moon, which was a counterpart to the cycle of human lifetime, and in the drawing the 15th night of the moon represented the 35th year of a person's lifetime, and was significant in that it represented the moon and sun in perfect balance.[4]

I was thirty-five years old, and things were moving very rapidly and profoundly for me at that time, for, as I said, I was finally grounded by the earth, and so the electrical energy of the spirit could move freely into me.

Also in Campbell's book was a description of a person's kundalini rising, which was another synchronicity, arriving to me in short order, due to the fact that during my time in the hut, without any effort or intention on my part, my own kundalini began to spontaneously rise up. This was a process which occurred over several weeks, and, despite various dreams and intuitions, I did not know what was happening until my heart chakra opened up in a burst of empathy, and then I could feel the serpent writhing within, passing up through my pineal gland, and heading for my crown.

Slowly, ever slowly, the serpentine energy had climbed its way up my chakras, while I changed nothing in my day to day life, eating what I always ate, drinking beer, smoking the occasional joint, and going mad with loneliness, wonder, confusion, and joy. Business as usual.

It was in those lower, grounded reelings, where I was cast about in my usual cataleptic fits of spiritual exhaustion, attempting relentlessly to escape myself that I was also sinking further and further into the filth and the flesh, and only because of this was I eventually …able to fly. Ah, to fly- to erupt without any movement, to rise without going high. I flew inside myself, through the infinite space of unmeaning, through the lift and the glide of just being.

I suddenly belonged to existence with such tangibility, such connection, such passion, that in that blessed bind I implausibly found a hidden release; as if I could not escape the flesh without becoming flesh completely; as if the context must devour the Word, in order for the contextless soul to go free.

Which is to say that I stopped *only* dreaming of the flesh, and I

---

[4] According to the book: "This is a moment of great mystical importance. Here your consciousness, your body and its consciousness, are at their prime." Joseph Campbell (*Transformation of Myth Through Time*, pg 26)

became *also* the flesh. I had to take on the flesh so as to take up the flesh, for the Assumption occurs when the flesh is assumed. And I, divested from the thought structures of mankind, entered into the bridal chamber where naked Beingness and naked Non-beingness unrecognized their differences and were unified into one.

The fact that I changed nothing in my life and had my kundalini awaken and rise of its own accord, makes me wonder if all the postures and purifications espoused by the so-called experts are as useless as every other piece of advice applauded and lauded by the back-slapping dilettantes so prevalent in the new age and spiritual industries these days.

In fact, I know of a woman whose kundalini rose up completely in a few minutes while she was at work and had never considered coaxing it forth. But forth it came, out of the root, up the spine, and blasted out the top of her head, which is how it ended for me, blowing out through the top of my head, which made me feel like I had no head, but was suddenly immersed in the entire consciousness of the unseparated cosmos, where the self becomes all, the *I* becomes everything, and nothing is distinguished from another for the division has ended with the disintegration of the wall.

It was a staggering openness which I experienced then, but which escaped from me soon afterwards, because, as I said, I had to leave the grounding of my little earth-floor hut, due to the bluffer, and fly back to Vancouver in the middle of winter, and suddenly my flesh was now separated from contact with the earth by impervious layers of pavement, concrete, wood, tile, rubber soles, and socks. My contact with the grounding Mother had been removed, and with that gone the winged serpent had nowhere to hold. A few weeks later I began experiencing excruciating pains along my spine, and then had a dream in which a huge snake was cut in half, and I knew then the peril of our distance from the earth, the ground, the Mother. My kundalini had risen, and then had been broken in two, and it would be a long while before that chakra energy had healed enough to send the little serpent writhing upward again.

Modern culture is so far removed from contact with the earth that it is no wonder we exist like frantic phantoms in an astral chaos, for there is no grounding in modern life, and without grounding- and by that I am being absolutely literal- without living upon, touching, and being one with the ground, the polarity of our possible wholeness is thrown way out of balance, and the spirit soars like a kite without a hold, a bird without a roost, and a ghost without a fleshy home.

I say this because never have I felt such otherworldly peace as I did in that hut, when I lived on and became intimate with this earth, this flesh, and this body which are one.

We must live in direct contact with the earth once again if the roots required by the wings are to hold. Roots and wings, these are the interdependent halves of our spiritualized earthly lives. For it is only in the loving and hallowing of the flesh and the earth that the spirit learns that it is not whole without it. And it is only in the voice of the flesh that the song of the spirit is finally sung.

*

fourteen

Spiritual processes have not always gone as smoothly for me as the unintentional rising of my kundalini. In fact, I would say that my path has often felt like I was trying to drive a child's tricycle along a mountain path covered with fallen trees, for, as much as I was embraced by the Mother, the spirit, and God in my hut in Hawaii, so also have I often been prodded and pushed around the world under not such comfortable circumstances as in that oasis in Babylon.

Like my ill-fated trip to France where, instead of being passionately embraced by the soul and body of the Parisian woman I was going to see, I received, as compensation, not only a bloodthirsty welcoming and instant heartbreak, but also a malicious beating by Christ, my baptism in water and spirit, a one day visit to Rome in which two prophecies a crazed friend of mine had uttered about my life came true, and gut-splitting intestinal cramps from fasting improperly during four bewildering days in Paris, going mad for love and hunger, all without knowing that the ruthless chastening sent down upon me at that time would not end until everything inside of me was dead except innocence.

Had I known at the outset of my journey to France that it would be fraught with nothing but madness, hunger, misery, absurdity, and loss, certainly I never would have gone. But then, neither would I have been murdered by the Man, baptized into eternity, and then resurrected as the virgin in a wholly new female trinity.

But let me explain. Oh, let me helplessly explain what is impossible to explain.

I had decided to go to France for a number of reasons, the most important of which was to rekindle a romance involving a Parisian woman, whom I had enjoyed a dazzling but brief tryst with a few years earlier, in North America, and who had supposedly welcomed me into her bosom whenever I felt ready to nest there.

I arrived in France and at first was feeling quite carefree and simply basking in the spirit and soul of the land and its people. I was quick to realize, in fact, that, in many ways, France had a very similar

50

feel to India. Perhaps because these countries are two of the rare areas on earth where the culture, and not just nature, is in harmony with the Mother, who is the presiding aspect of the Godhead in both places.

Indeed, you can feel Her in France, in the mood of the city parks, in the ancient statues and architecture, and in the citizen's uninhibited sensuality, which left me thoroughly aghast on my first trip to France, a decade earlier, when I had seen young couples rolling about on the lawn of a city park, unabashedly groping, French-necking, and otherwise doing everything but public coitus with each other, in broad daylight, without a hint of care or concern for the thousands of other park attendees. Nothing like that goes on in North America. Oh, no, better to be properly shaved, dressed, and well-behaved, at all times, despite the primordial needs and desires running amok within each one of us, so as not to let the others know the wild animal lurking manically within.

But in France there is no division between beast, man, and God. All occur without obstruction within each individual. It is a land of cultured barbarians, of urban Pagans, as I came to call them on my second trip there- when I felt the Mother's energy so strongly that I thought I was back in India. Though maybe I was just undergoing a sentient premonition of all that was to follow on my unwitting pilgrimage into the whore of Babylon's underbelly.

Looking back now I realize that my dance with the Dark Mother began long before I had any knowledge of Her, or of the history of Kali in India, or the Black Madonna in France, though this is where I would find myself, caught in Her hallucinatory clutches, broken apart into a thousand unrecognizable pieces, and then reassembled into a wobbling new thing, as I succumbed to the love and violence of Her and Her vicious Son. Had I known, two years prior to this, what eating a chocolate Madonna in a dream might portend, I may have up and quit the whole quest I didn't know I was inexorably launched upon.

But now I was in France, on a train heading into the southern Alps, on my way to visit another Mary- the young Parisian flower whom I had come all the way to France to see, so as to continue our wonderful and yet distant relationship. But it was not to be, for the Mother and Son duo of disaster and delight had other plans, as I came to find out in the throes of the etherical delirium I was soon to enter in upon.

It happened that, having fallen asleep on the train running from Paris to the French Alps, where my mistress awaited, I dreamt that a madman in dreadlocks was chasing after me with a shotgun, shooting and killing me, over and over again, as I fled frantically, was shot, died, got back up, fled, was shot, died, and rose again. The madman was Christ, and I was his game, and when finally I was finished- dead and yet still living- the dream shifted and I had a vision

51

of Christ showing me how to eventually rise out from underneath water, to etherealize, and then to disappear. It was a teaching about the true nature of death and resurrection.

But now I was dead, and I arrived at my lover's house, a little less than fully together, and she must have sensed sublimely that she was now being courted by a cadaver rather than a mountain man- a recognition which soon turned that tender, caring doe into a vicious bear, no longer willing to be eaten, but instead bent on devouring me as carrion. Which is another way of saying that in the energy shift accompanying my spiritual destruction and awaiting rebirth, my mistress had somehow changed from a dream into a nightmare. And it is a horrible day when you are both murdered by Christ and betrayed by your lover's kiss, but that is what happens when the tunnel you are walking through is no longer a part of your path, and the mad chastener arrives to chase you mercilessly the other way.

So I soon left her and the Alps, like a specter dragging his own loveless corpse behind him, and trained back to Paris, and in a frantic attempt to right my floundering ship …I began to fast.

Fasting is one of the most demented mortifications I had ever previously undertaken, albeit rarely at that, but fasting in Paris was a step further into insanity and masochism, for soon enough I was a moveable salivary gland wandering about ghoulishly amidst the moveable feast. There is nowhere on earth where food is displayed in markets, shop windows, and cafés, as temptingly as it is in Paris. And that this had been the chosen venue for my self-inflicted flagellation shows the extent of my contorted inner condition, brought on by Christ's brutal attack upon my existence.

I remained four torturous days in Paris, and never ate a thing. *Quel idiot!*

I was running away from myself, then towards myself, towards, and away, forward and backward, everywhere and none. I was separate and yet not separate, for I was in a tug-of-war between losses, where heaven, hell, and earth met like an improvised patch in the fabric of being, inside my weary, radiant core; as if being torn in all directions by a band of lunatics, I was painfully going nowhere.

On the fifth day I boarded a train for the Riviera, and began eating fruit. I was headed to Rome- a destination which I cannot remember the reasons for choosing, though I know there must have been reasons, for I was in the grip of the Dark Lady and her ruthless Son, and His bullets were still flying after me, and my fate was well described by their invisible hands. I stopped en route to spend the night in Nice, staggered feebly to a hill-top hostel, went to my bed, fell asleep, and awoke next morning so clean, so hollow, and so open and alive, that I could feel the Mother's heart beat within me, with an intimacy and power that I had never felt from that subterranean rhythm before, nor after, for now She had taken me back into her bosom, as a Mother does after the thrashing, and I was in Her, and She was in me, and the whole world throbbed to the beat of Her love, life, and sorrow.

Perhaps this was the Mother's way of comforting me, and so now She and Her Son were playing good-cop, bad-cop with me: one of them laying on the whip and steel, and the other holding me finally to Her chest. Oh, She is a dark consort to the vicious Man at times, but thankfully, as I said, She has in Her what all mother's have in them after the spanking, which is to say- love.

Thus I lay there basking in that thick and engulfing energy and unquestionable connection, sensing that I was completely within Her, as we all are, and that the very pulse of Her heart *was* my existence. I lay there, receiving the integral energy of that lower communion, and when I was finally calmed I slowly arose out of bed, and, after eating my first breakfast in five days, left the hostel whereupon I instantly met an angel sent to ease my way.

It was a spontaneous encounter, just outside the dorm, where I struck up a conversation with a middle-aged German woman who was also forsaken by love, was also following her dreams- which were truer than reality- was also engaged in an austere diet, and was also in France pursuing a tragic love, although her passion was directed towards a perfume tycoon whom she was certain had been her husband in many previous lives- a fact which he acknowledged after meeting her, though at the time of our meeting she, like I, was also being led about into the hotbed of loss and confusion due to the divine intent, no doubt, to simplify a self-imposed problematic existence.

She and I were perfect mirrors for each other, because All is reflected in all, and, as it is said, whatever comes to you in life is a reflection of what is inside of you.[5]

In the two hours which we spent together we covered every topic or inner issue we could reach, from ancient Egypt- where she claimed to have been Nefertiti- to the Apocalypse. She was a breath of cosmic air blown into my asphyxiated lungs, and I inhaled her vigorously. In fact, I had found such comfort with her that I began to share the spiritual turmoil I had encountered over the last few weeks, including the dream of Christ murdering me and then of Him rising out of the water. To this she nonchalantly remarked- "That was your baptism," a statement which did not sound necessarily correct to me,

---

[5] This 'mirroring' aspect of the external world exists up until the point when the spirit within a person comes to live at a greater pace than the manifest can keep up with. That is when the reciprocity of the universe falls lame, for now the person is living ahead of the drama, which follows them like a wake follows a boat, and therefore the manifest can no longer be used like an external mirror to gauge internal growth, because the person has become the living Life within, and nothing outward can keep up with it.

but was corroborated by an ex-minister friend of mine, a month later back in Canada.[6]

But for now I was still drowning in the lower waters, and still unable to rise out and fly.

I parted from the Egyptian Queen a little more at peace, a little more faithful, a little more 'together'- as the colloquial expression applicably denotes- and then departed for Rome.

South I went into Italy, on an overnight train, out of France, out of the land of cultured barbarians, out of the home of the Dark Mother, and down into Roma- *amor*- where the Father and Mother still are one.

It was in Rome where I was shown that even though I felt lost and confused, love-sick and weary, and was still wandering about like a husk of chaff devoid of meal, blown about in the arid wind with no possibility of setting root, I was, as ever, being guided and healed.

I noted this as I entered the Sistine Chapel, and looked up at the plates Michelangelo had spent four years prone in the making, and quickly recognized the plate in which God is creating man- the one where God's and man's fingers are coming together to touch. This was a revelation for me, because at the moment I saw it I was mentally transported back to Canada, where, two months earlier, I had been visiting a buddy in the hospital who had, according to the establishment, lost his mental stability, but who was in fact dwelling in a heavenward realm, all the while spouting gibberish and prophetic insights like the Oracle of Delphi gone mad. Only he wasn't mad, he was in the loving arms of the Lord, and he was spouting the Word, and the Word became flesh, and my buddy reached out his finger towards me, and I reached out mine towards him, and we touched I didn't know why until I stood there in the Sistine Chapel, two mad months later, broken and mended, abandoned and found, destroyed and created in the fantastic, centrifugal vortex of heaven's quickening hurricane.

*

fifteen

The denouement of that European chastening and baptism came like a slow and excruciating climax which did not culminate until a number of weeks later, after I had left that disastrous continent

---

[6] Many years later I read somewhere that St. Patrick had received his revelations and 'Christing' in dreams.

behind, had flown back to the west coast of North America, and was holed up in a lonely room in San Francisco, still battered, broken, and bruised, despite now knowing that all was as it should be.

It was here, finally, that I had come to be like a flesh bag of dissipated spiritual fragments from which a new cornerstone could be chosen, and from that rock another temple could be born. And by that I mean that during my stay on the west coast of America, I was eventually liberated from the ardors of my transformation which had been set in motion by the murderous Man, but this end came about only after I had abandoned the torturous confines of conception, false conception, and arrived at the emancipating qualities of immaculate conception, otherwise known as ignorance, thus bringing me back again to the center of my own eternal wheel.

This came about, as I said, while I was staying in San Francisco, for though I desperately wanted to return to Vancouver and the welcoming arms of my buddies, I couldn't budge any further, because I was a cracked vessel and had nothing to meet or greet them with except a look of desperation- a desperation which nothing but mercy could help me through, and so I knew that I could not return until the inner apocalypse was over. So I stayed in San Francisco, exhausting every last iota of mental energy, trying to put some of the pieces that had fallen apart back together, so that I might return to life again, somehow. The battle had gone on for weeks and I could see no end to it and so I made the drastic decision to leave the city on foot, and head up the coastal highway, and walk the worm and torment out of me, even if I had to walk all the way to Vancouver.

Such a firm resolution must have been the catalyst required for the climax to come, because the night prior to my departure I had gone to bed in psychological tatters, had begged for mercy, and then dreamt a dream in which many female bodies were lying on many tables in a morgue, all of whom had been murdered. At one of the tables a woman physician- whom afterward I was to call Physis- was working frantically, attempting to resurrect one of the bodies. Beside her a solicitous wise woman- whom, upon waking, I was to call Sophia- was in a grievous panic, worrying that the resurrection would not be successful. Finally Physis moved back from the table and pronounced that the job was finished, and that she had been triumphant. Yet Sophia was still absolutely overwrought with anxiety, and was beseeching Physis, asking her if she was certain the woman was alive. At that moment a young, very innocently minded girl- whom later I was to call the Virgin- sat upright on the table and playfully said- "Of course I'm OK", and I awoke.[7]

---

[7] I recognize now that this dream was much more than just a personal transformational event; it also displayed to me the missing pieces to the six-pointed star, a symbol which links the upper with the lower trinity, thus completing the cosmos. That is, whereas the

This was the type of transformational dream which would occur to me every now and then, when the tension of growth and change into something new- because the old me was no longer useful to the whole- had reached its breaking point, like a child who had been forced to wear the same clothes year after year despite his growing body, until either the flesh became contorted or the seams tore apart and the garments were lost to the wind. I was scattered to the wind that evening, at the climax of the struggle, and all that remained was all that can ever remain during a complete transformation- innocence. I had become as a child.

I knew then that everything inside of me, except wonder, had been destroyed during the previous weeks, because I had fallen into a false view of reality- and only the unknowing, virginally minded child could remain within me, were I to get back to the hub. I had been wiped clean in the fires leading up to the genocide and resurrection. And now, sitting awake, I felt an amazing calm and joy come over me, for I had come again to the blessed experience of awe- to the place where I did not know anything.

I had been caught in a labyrinth of my own creation, and to get me out of it the Dark Mother and her Dark Son had to come brutally after me, and all the walls had to come down about me, for I could not find my way out until after the earthquake- when finally I was free in the open space of pure and blessed ignorance again. Everything had been solved by killing every solution. And that morning I aborted my now unnecessary mad march up the rainy coast, jumped on a bus, and headed home.

*

sixteen

I returned to Vancouver, after the resurrection in San Francisco, and once again stood innocent before mankind, because I had done my time, had been scoured inside with Christ's caustic soda, and had come out of the flames tempered, glowing, and refreshingly free.

Indeed, it was only after the grosser movements of my confined imagination had been burned clean of redundancy and need;

---

upper-trinity (and I use the terms upper and lower without value judgment) consists of the Father, the Son, and the Holy Ghost, the lower-trinity consists of Sophia, Physis, and the Virgin, otherwise known as the wise female archetype, feminine matter, and the openness of female concavity.

after the unforgiving calamities usurped me from all courage and despair; after the whole mad show boiled up in ecstasy and failure; after I stumbled and bloomed, aghast and transparent in what could not be and is; it was then that I broke, redeemed and abolished, as if newly awoken or just fallen to sleep; it was then that I possessed intimacy with gratitude and awe, because I was life and living, and now was all too new forever.

Like a happenstance dismay of unknown wonders, the specious and soothing images upon which I had been weaned had broken apart in an apocalypse of unmeaning. And it was from, and because of, such a disastrous undoing- in which I was dismantled into unrecognized bits and then smashed irrevocably beyond myself- that I was subsequently patched back together, so as to return to the world, to life, and somehow manage to live it. And that is the hard and living hell of it, let me tell you.

Euphoria, you see, is indeed a ghastly blessing; I expired from the inspirations by which I was engulfed, I was dispersed by the ecstasies which described me, I exploded against the firmament, and then was torn asunder, shredded magnanimously into digestible bits, and swallowed back into the fulcrum of torturous, graced bewilderments. I lived then intoxicated by a thousand realms at once, respirating in the thin abysses.

There are indeed limitless depths of disbelief which I have swum through breathlessly; the incontrovertible, exhilarating moments when I remembered that I did not understand.

My mind had become a lung through which I inhaled impossibilities. My endurance was infinite. Never did I feel the need to surface gasping, for I had come again to live in the impunity of not-knowing (ergo in the redemption of awe), and I knew that every moment in which I would not stare incapably off into space, aghast with disbelief- every moment in which I was not honest enough to seize up, inexorably baffled, every moment that my being did not turn incorrigibly towards the splendor of the unreachable, immanent Mecca that is and is not mind- would be a golden moment lost.

I sought to last forever in those ephemeral cataclysms, in those lost velocities and spent configurations, wherein I was composed solely of problematic ecstasies, of masochistic ebullience, for I so willingly inhabit only those disastrous tranquilities, expatiating along the harrowing, vertiginous ridge of lostness, and thus thriving fecund in those dimensions which exhaust me.

It was not enlightenment that I underwent, but its opposite; a pure, absolute, intelligent ignorance. Who are we? Why are we? What are we? I tell you I did not, and do not know. I only know that we are not what we think we are, thus we are what we are not. Hallelujah indeed!

I had returned again to the mystery, the distillate, the quintessence of the all.

As the last remnant of memory and recognition dissipated from my dissipating consciousness I was delivered into unimaginability after unimaginability; I received a showering of 'never beforeness' colliding all about and around me.

There are no samples nor tastes of infinity, there are only unswallowable gulps of life, drowning me in swollen breaths of intobated non-suffocation. Me? and this? and all of it, and good God how to come to terms?!

How could it be? How could all of this be? And yet ...and yet it is, and I am it- the Mystery incarnate within itself; intimate and detached, part and yet parcel of the whole crazy show, as it were.

I no longer yearn for fathomable happenings. This world is as good a place as any to confront implausibility. I know merely a bewildering, spectacular, authenticity that I can but poorly describe as 'unfathomableness'- a confounding, wordless, somethingness; I believe only in the outlandishness of being; I am convincingly, absolutely, absorbed by the wonderment of being.

My life becomes more and more mythical to me; I come to realize that I am not what I am; I am less and so much more; I contain everything that was, is, and will be; every event, every fantasy, every reality. I am, and I cannot believe it.

Everyday, reality becomes increasingly less real, and this unreality becomes increasingly more real; the unreality of reality feels more real. Reality is so unreal it must be real; absurdity is the most certain validation of our questionable existence.

It is not logical to see the world logically. The reality of reality is its unrealness; reality is nothing more than the unrealness that it is; a fantasy that is real. Reality occurs as this unreality of the real- as simply the most absurd concoction of improbabilities that a reasoning mind can hope to withstand. It is far beyond anything imaginable; whatever it is- it *is*; and only reality could have come up with this unreality.

Ah, to be the complexity that man is, and yet to not be complex enough to understand this very complexity; existence pondering existence; mystery mystified by mystery; it amazes me that I 'am', and yet that I do not, by the very act of being, know of it already.

Have I then come into this life only so as to applaud the miraculous implausibility of all that is, by ecstatically not understanding it? Am I here to humbly exalt the glorious mystery of being, and nothing more? Are there others who have lost their mind as grace-fully as me?

Yes, indeed, Prometheus may have stolen the fire, but I made off with the bomb. I severed the bonds by which I was uselessly

58

tethered to machination. I slayed the last of a dying species by debunking plausibility, and disproving without proving.

I uprooted the Tree of Knowledge, and then burned the fruit using the limbs for a pyre.

I resonated entropy into the tangling forms, tearing all of life's hardened images from my virginal eyes, and finally I forgot the knowledge by which I had been ex-communicated from Life. And when I staggered back onto my feet and found my new footing in the ether- that was the first step I ever took forward.

It was as if I finally caught up to myself, and then ...I existed no longer. As if I descended and then rose again, resurrecting myself out of the death of what I know I was not, into what I know not; no, I do not know what it was that I was, nor what it is that I am- and this is the cornerstone of my absorption.

I did not, after all, contaminate my being in the vortex of plausibility. I did not embrace the rhetorical overtures of conception. I did not accept life's eternal distractions. My task was, and is, to continually not-know what others claim to know; to weigh the anchors of the mind.

I have no truths, only the rejection of all untruths. I did not find a conclusion, only a beginning; I disappeared into mystery, emerging out of the absence of myself.

Yea indeed, as the raging forms glistened in the ecstasy of what may, I stood again before myself.

Indeed, it is time to purge the cloaca of our fetid concepts; time to cauterize our septic meanderings; time to euthanize obsolete symbologies. After all I have seen, and all I have unseen, I now preen conception from my mind like a baboon picking squirming gnats from its own knotted fur; I gnaw upon the mind's maggots.

I simply want to erase everything and to start anew; to smash the blackboards, and throw away the chalk. Oh, life indeed is a more genuine mystery than it is a common fact.

I am no longer a coward of the mind, I will not cognitively submit to agreeable notions. I unknow the world ...defiantly.

In a genocide of cerebrations I massacre ontologies and pillage their existential remains, ruthlessly exterminating ideas, and hacking my way through the barricades of false emancipations. For in the realm of false understandings there is no heroism, only a war that never ceases, and soldiers that never die.

You see, though mine was a distorted illumination; like the blinding light of the sun, bouncing off the lightless, light-giving moon, I did still rise up in the night of our being, and shine forth despite my perpetual darkness.

And now I have returned to take mankind's whole being away with a single malicious observance.

59

Give me your greatest edifice, man, that I may with innocence knock it mercilessly to the ground.

I did not come to take part, but to take apart. Mine is a ruinous decomprehension. I have devoured facts, and excreted mystery; sacrificing so as to get rid of- and not with intent to gain- I did not cauterize the infected wound, I severed the entire limb; I unrecognized existence in a fanatical moment of destructive non-interpretation. I am a wild animal of mind. I am ferocious in brave ecstasy. I am savage ...because I am free. The blood of meaning is on my hands.

*

seventeen

Why did this whole crazy show come about? I do not know. I know only that it came about.

It was as if I lived a manic descent from unbeing into being; I did not understand, nor control my harrowing plunge. But when I landed I hit with a thud that would have killed me if the Self wasn't an undying being. That is how I was able to get back up and walk onward, wiped clean-through by the flames of my agonizing re-entry. And when that happens- when the kenosis has come full circle, and you're alive and dead, alien and belonging, strong and yet broken- that is when the real work begins. That is when you bring the fire back to earth- acquired for the men who will misunderstand you, stolen from the powers who will despise even your good. So be it.

I say this because, like many of you, I also had my insides ripped out, hacked to pieces, molded into nothing recognizable, and stuffed back into my groaning hollow. Loss and sadness were nothing new to my eternal being. But all movements have a reckoning, a consummation, and a respite, for the moving moment is alive, and grows and transforms just as any organism grows- imperceptibly, slowly and yet continually, and just as relief comes to a fugitive finally brought down after an arduous flight, so does this mad show run down its engine, and is fulfilled or is finished with a sigh of delight.

Yea indeed, like a dizzy logotrope, spinning wildly about, grasped by that halcyon light which follows the passionate arc- to turn towards the colossal mystery of being, to follow the real but invisible movements, to want truth inside of you more than you even want yourself there, is to appear mad and sane in the world of reason. To move with a heaven-tethered eye, never bending from its sight, is to look through a different window, and yet still live inside the house.

I had spent much of my life trying to pretend that I was not

60

lost, until I finally realized that everyone is lost, and that the whole mad show is nothing but a card-house of hiding places which people build so as to forget all about this absurdity, because a person becomes deranged trying to belong to something they do not understand. And no one understands.

And so I eventually accepted that to be lost is to be honest, and that therefore it is not wrong to howl wildly into the lonely night, for there are no remaining options but to go mad with ecstasy and anguish, to fall in love with the night, and to find the gratitude in which to live the mystery out.

But am I not also caught in the inexorable, powerful grip of life? Yes indeed I am also caught, and yet ...I am also that very grip; that grip squeezed in upon itself like an empty fist, unable to break free of its clench until it punches something harder. But I do not punch. I only grip more arduously into myself, because only exhaustion will undo my hold upon my task, my world, my self. I am the grip on life, of life, in life, but I do not punch ...I sing.

I too am in this world, this life, this voice behind the mind. I am speaking slowly, through the misty night of our old losses, hoarse from the brooding depths of life's fatigued untruth. I pause often, sigh, and continue. Hear my hollow metronome, charmed of the meter's dark whimper.

I thought of never touching down, of never saying who I was, where I had been, or what I did when I got here.

I thought of never writing a syllable from this broken mold of unwhole timelessness, because it seemed that I had attained nothing: no happiness, no truth, no love, no answer. I had no path to salvation, and no idea of how to redeem. I had nothing to give others but myself, and my wild, euphoric imaginings.

But life brings its own tasks, and I am not one to argue. Not, at least, with the One who yet knows me.

Were it not for the frequent bouts of absolute catatonia, interspersed with durations of uncontrollable imbecilic laughter, I should say it was not all worth it. But I was not born from the lineage of complaint. I harbor no existential vendettas. In the end I did not deplore the insurmountable perplexity, nor was I thanklessly discouraged by it. Though neither have I bled endlessly through the wound of consciousness for nothing; for if I have stuck my earnest spirit out from the warm abyss only for long enough to spill forth my bile and laughter then, as now, while the roaring blade hastens whistling towards its mark, I shall not miss a beat, nor a word, nor a jingle, but will calmly wail out my true song, my vision, my life.

And so, under the coercion of the tender, tickling Muse do I send out my own imperfect vision into the barbaric land of men, and the Word, while it is alive and living, emits from my diffident pen.

But if I share with you what I can, it is not so as to impose a regiment upon our infinite lives, but only so that I might give myself away, in a blind attempt to join with you completely.

Oh, perhaps I am only a hoarse voice in the chaotic chorus of the Great Song, but ...I am a voice. And though what I have to say is only what I have seen, I cannot help but seek to quicken our spirits through a vortex of awe and gratitude, and so to bleed the voice of sorrow from the stone.

And yet, am I simply a lame busker, crooning stale requiems at the honored gates, to all those gathered impatiently about, waiting to be denied entry? Am I but the phlegmatic sexton of an abandoned, crumbling, obsolete temenos? A bell-ringer without a church? A hanged man, ejaculating life back at his dead executioners?

No, no, definitely not, for I am still alive and free, and though I did not begin to fight until I had already surrendered, that was when I became undefeatable, because though I was the weakest man alive ...no one could destroy me. But before I got there I had to suffer through the consequences of the lie; I had to lose myself in order to become myself; I had to descend to the Devil, before I could rise to God. And then what came to me in the tender futility of life's beauty, as I balanced solicitously between exaltation and rage, was a tepid, graceful bewilderment- a melancholy born of beauty, despair, and wonder, which caused me in the end to only vehemently affirm life, to embrace everything, to take it all up, all of it, to accept, and accept, and accept, until there was nothing left of me but acceptance; to not struggle towards, to not struggle away; to be willing to say "Yes, yes, of course ...yes!", even if that 'yes' agreed to the 'no' that was the very disintegration of itself, so that in that surge of dynamic affirmation, the flood of unbiased acceptance would rush through the estuary of my being, and, like a dam broken above a village, would cause all souls caught within my ubiquity to be swept away from all comfort, all knowledge, all pain, and then to be gathered up, drowned in a torrent of rapture and glee, taken away by the new tide, and swept out to the welcoming sea.

*

PART II:
SERVING THE SON

"And now they saw that the Christ had died to the Sun, died cosmically to the Sun, had been given by the Father, to be born on Earth, to die and descend to the ends of the earth where the Father could not reach, and to rise again, so that his life and the Father's and the Holy Spirit's could become one with the earth itself and all it contained."
Christopher Bamford

"Split a piece of wood and I am there. Lift up the stone, and you will find me there."
Jesus, the Christ: Gospel of Thomas

one

To be spiritually initiated, as I was initiated in France, by the unexpected violence of Christ and the Motherly discipline of Mary, is to be recruited as a foot soldier into a war in which you can never tell who's on your side, you can never find enough ammunition, and you can only win by losing yourself.

I was sent on a tour of duty to New Zealand, the orders of which came in one dream: I dreamt that my father owned a banana plantation in that country. A simple dream, and one which Jungians or other symbolists would no doubt tear apart and massacre into a tepid message bound up in historical archetypes and mythology. But this was no alchemical dream.[8] For I had already recognized many times before that when I dreamt of my father, this was actually the male aspect of the Godhead communicating to me, and when I dreamt of my mother it was the female aspect. So, my father had a banana plantation in New Zealand. I was therefore bound for that destination, without question. Except first I had to correct the simple problem that I was penniless, a factor which was fixed in short order as I was guided to quickly earn enough money for the journey.[9]

I arrived in Auckland, spent a few days on the nearby coast, then met up with my *soror*, who had flown in a few days after me, and together we hitchhiked out to the Coromandel Peninsula, so as to get away from the madding crowd as quickly as possible. After camping out uneventfully that first evening, we had our thumbs out again in the morning and were picked up by a multi-tattooed, rum-sipping, young renegade named Jim, who lived and worked in the area, had fathered four kids, and was on a weekend drive-about and binge while his wife and family were away elsewhere. He looked as tough as they come, but was as soft as a feather inside. Jim drove us down the coast a ways, and then let us off at a beach where we planned to hang about and camp that evening. However, after staying in the area for a few hours, the

---

[8] As much as I appreciate Jung and the entire dream-interpretation movement, the cosmos is far fuller, far more intertwined, invisible, intimate, and intelligent than can be explained by boiling everything down into archaic messages from the common unconscious. It takes only one astral journey for an individual to realize that conventional dream theory is absolutely inadequate to deal with the hinterland of sleep. The universe is alive and conscious, and far beyond what certain limiting understandings will ever allow us to admit.

[9] The ways in which I was guided to make such money, wherein there was no doubt that the invisible hand was choreographing the whole show, are described in my earlier book, *In, and Of*.

soror and I decided it wasn't a place we wanted to camp, and so we walked back up to the road and stuck our thumbs out again. After waiting a short while a car came racing towards us and squealed to a halt. It was Jim again. He had driven a full loop around the area, just for the joy of it, and so once again we were in his buggy and heading south. I suppose Jim and I had found some comfort together by this time, and had located some common ground on which to converse, for we began discussing all sorts of fringe experiences including magic mushroom trips, and the play of the spirit on earth. And it was near the end of this second drive together, as we were approaching our next destination, that I decided to query Jim as to whether he knew anyone in the area who owned a banana patch. He said he knew of only one- his parents.

Ah yes, the spirit was with us- as if there was ever any doubt- for the spirit runs the whole show, and is the show, and no matter how obscure or impossible the odds, no matter how confused or disoriented we become trying to follow it, the guiding spirit is always with us, no matter what is going on, nor how chaotic or vague, we are always where we should be.

By the time we had ascertained that serendipitous piece of information about Jim's parents, however, the evening was upon us, and it was too late to proceed on the quest, so the *soror* and I said goodnight to Jim, and he sped off on his merry way, and we went to a nearby campsite.

The next day the *soror* and I turned around and, following Jim's directions to his parents, hitched back up the coast in the direction which we had just come the day before, arriving at his folks humble little homestead in the late morning.

Upon meeting them I was certain that I had found the intent of my sublime mission, for Jim's parents turned out to be tremendously gentle, unobtrusive, generous, and meek folks. That is, they were children of God- the one who sent me, the one who harbors the outcasts, the impoverished, and the lonely. And Jim's parents were doing just the same, as I was to find out, for they had created over many years, without riches, a safe haven for a fare number of dispossessed and homeless souls. Which is to say, they were doing God's work on earth.

To be sure, they were no bible-thumping holier-than-thou types. In fact, the four of us never even spoke a word of religion between us. And I gathered, if I had to generalize, that these folks were influenced by Buddhism, marijuana, and gardening, more than anything else, and may never have even read nor heard of the Bible, or may have considered it absolute balderdash for all I know. But they had love in their hearts, and that, after all, is the only true religion.

So the *soror* and I spent the afternoon with Jim's parents, and

65

the four of us had some lovely conversation and communion, thus connecting our spirits through the eyes and, as such, remaining together even after parting. And that, I expect, was the intent of my sublime directive- to meet those meek and honest owners of the banana patch, and link souls with them.[10] For in the act of meeting others at the soft and intimate essence of our separate cores, the consciousness of God within each of us comes into recognition of its divided parts, which, upon that recognition, are no longer divided. Thus the many become one.

Furthermore, after leaving those beatific folks, our stay in New Zealand came to provide a great wealth of cosmic and alchemical experiences for me, most of which are either incredibly difficult, or impossible to describe, for certain events in life are so unique and intimate with an individual's exclusive path that the profundity and impact of such experiences cannot be related nor given to another- because they are intended for no other. I can only say, therefore, in a very imperfect way, that traveling to New Zealand, and to the southern hemisphere for the first time in my life, was like moving to a completely new vantage point in the earthly drama, and, as such, seeing it from a different perspective altogether.[11]

On that trip I was to meet individuals who told impressive tales of their meetings with 'masters', such as Jesus; I met folks who claimed to have been healed by aliens, and others who had spent decades on Mt. Shasta, studying the 'I AM' teachings of both the masters and aliens. I also met, on the south island, one of my sisters who came from the same limb of the Tree of Life as myself, and who

---

[10] "...that also he should gather together in one the children of God that were scattered abroad." John 11:52

[11] For example, I was to discover on that trip that the earth itself is a living, hologromatic whole in which aspects of the earth are mirrored through itself, inverted, and contorted, and shot out somewhere else on the globe. Such understandings came about because I began to recognize the similarities between New Zealand and the much smaller Queen Charlotte Islands, off the coast of western Canada: both Archipelagos are composed of two main islands, both have large sand-spits running off the north end, both have fiord-like areas on the south west side of the southern island, and both have a reasonable sized island in the very south. The island is Stewart Island in New Zealand, and Kunghit Island in the Charlottes, which, interestingly enough, is separated from the southern main island by Huston-*Stewart* Channel.

This kind of holistic observation will be hard to stomach for most people who require hardened facts. No matter, I point this out to those who are willing to bend their perspectives enough to see the possibility that the earth is a living entity, and, furthermore, is an orb whose living circumference is reflected through its core, and therefore, just as in the spiritual realm, everything in the material realm is mirrored in and through all else. All is reflected in all.

was not only a member of my physical sister's spiritual archetype[12], but was also so connected to the minutiae of my own life that we had a vast array of mundane occurrences in common: like the fact that she had begun playing the recorder at the same time as I, just weeks before our meeting, and she had, I was to find out, pinned onto her office wall the exact three short pieces of inspired writing that I had been carrying with me, and occasionally handing out to acquaintances whom I thought might enjoy them.[13]

These types of 'coincidental' similarities are regular occurrences for souls lying close to one another at the epicenter of the creative core, regardless of their distance from each other on earth. Just as it has been found that identical twins, having been separated at birth, who find each other as adults, often have an implausible number of similar occurrences and interests in their lives; so it is the same with the subtle essence of spiritual siblings, who may know nothing of each other, but are still inspired from the same center, and therefore often share many commonalities, both sacred and profane.

In addition to all of the above, on that trip to New Zealand something was being worked out for, or between, my *soror* and myself. Something hidden, unconscious, or dark.

There are manifold reasons for me stating this, but only a few of which can be related, for these alone had cohesion in the manifest.

For example, my *soror* eventually purchased a used car while we were in New Zealand, so that we could tour the south island without the agony of further hitchhiking. She acquired it from a fellow who bought and sold cars to travelers as a way of making his daily keep. The interesting thing was this- not only did she have a prophetic dream of the exact car we ended up taking, but, a few days earlier I had dreamt that a debt, or penalty, had to be paid, for the killing of six people. Whether this was a purely symbolic, alchemical, transformative, karmic, vicarious, or penitential dream- to this day I do not know, but I do know that the car we drove away with- the one my *soror* had a preconceptual dream about- had the license plate K1ll 06, on it. Not likely a coincidence, not in my life anyway, and not a great

---

[12] There is a detailed description of spiritual archetypes in my book *In, and Of*. Briefly, however, a spiritual archetype is the underlying essence of a person, and this essence is the same in anyone belonging to the same common soul, just as, physiologically, all people of European stock are Caucasoid, and all those of African stock are Negroid, and so on. However, the spiritual archetype is an inner, eternal essence, to which individuals residing on the same branch of the Tree of Life belong, and of which they are unique expressions, or, types of the arche-types, as it were.

[13] Oriah Mountain Dreamer's *The Invitation*, Nelson Mandela's inaugural speech, and Goethe's classic quote on commitment.

omen to boot.

We spent much of the next six weeks touring the south island in that odd chariot, and guerrilla camping on the most remote beaches we could find, all the while throwing our spirits into each other- as is the way of the alchemical partnership- and then resurrecting each other out of the ruins.

We were also at this time practicing the sublime art of spiritually witnessing each other, by which we would sit face to face, at a distance of four or five feet from each other, and then soften and yet focus our separate gazes, away from the material realm and into the spiritual, and so see what was happening within the essence of the other. It was a tremendous esoteric art which we were learning from only our own internal intuition and guidance, but which would lead us down a path towards a vision neither of us expected, nor desired to see.

It happened that we had chosen a wild and distant beach just south of the town of Haast, my namesake, in which to enter the year 2000- the millennium changeover. We were alone out there but for a couple of charming little Blue penguins, and a swarm of not-so-charming sand flies, which is a common insult on New Zealand shores. And so we had retreated into our tent, deep in the woods, and had entered into the sublime seeing art when the horrors unfolded.

I expect that there was some fairly dark energy in the ether over the entire globe that evening, what with thoughts of apocalypse, armageddon, apokatastasis, and the second-coming roaming with wild abandon through the consciousness of six billion people, and into the common unconscious sea linking us all. But whether the *soror* and I had picked up a communal wave length, or were perceiving our own hidden demons, I do not know, but I do know that at the peak of stillness and subtle penetration required of the art we both disappeared from each other's sight, and all that remained was ...the Beast. I say this with absolute, categorical literalism. What lay before me, and before my *soror*, as she later expressed, was the inexplicable, undeniable vision of a fur-covered, crazed, wild, angry, and animalistic Beast. If you have seen the character created in recent renditions of *Beauty and the Beast*- a story which is nothing more than the metaphorical drama about the duality which lies within all of us- you will know *exactly* what we saw, in, and through the other. Quite a millennium shift, let me tell you.

As I say, I do not claim to understand the exact nature of our visions; whether we were meeting only the inner beast possessed by the *soror* and I- hence the K1ll 06 vehicle- or the repressed beast which lurks in the common unconscious and therefore belongs to all of us. To be sure, I have certainly found no shortage of darkness within myself, when I have been honest enough to take actual account. I have found aggression, deceit, violence, avarice, and lovelessness within myself,

68

which are facts I do not admit proudly, but only for the sake of telling it like it is. For since all things are clear in the sight of heaven, it matters little whether I come forth with such admittances or not, for all actions and thoughts are well documented in the ledgers above. I admit to these heinous characteristics only because in admitting to them do I hope to weaken them, and so to cause less division, destruction, and despair in the future.

Much of these agonies of which I speak come down to one, and only one, crucial flaw within myself: judgment. It is my judgment of others which has caused great division, my judgment of others which has caused me to destroy, and my judgment which has brought despair.

And so I pray, Lord, let me no longer create despair nor loneliness, unless it be Thy bidding. Let me bring but love and rapture, and let me celebrate the day. Let me hold, and heal, and forgive them, as they must hold, and heal, and forgive me. Let me kiss, admire, accept, and release them.

Lord, let me bring them home.

*

two

All is reflected through all. All is all.

I suppose, therefore, it was appropriate that I suffered for love, like I had never suffered before, a year or so after that trip to New Zealand, on the only island on earth, to my limited knowledge, where the Mother and Father- our cosmic parents- had gone to war, divided forces, and destroyed, in the violence of their combat, an entire civilization- Santorini, one of the many possible locations of lost Atlantis. Santorini, the island remains of a once giant Mediterranean volcano, and the ancient site, perhaps, of one of the Mother's most aggressive assaults upon the Father's creation- his prized civilization in the middle of the sea- the *medi-terra-nean* sea.

My esoteric findings lead me to surmise that Atlantis, as a culture, had grown too far away from wholeness, utilizing only the mind, and its logic, as a means of living on the earth, and, as had happened to its diametrically opposed twin, Lemuria- which had existed in the middle of the Pacific, and which used only the heart, and its emotions, as a guide- it could not sustain such one-sided existence in a universe striving for wholeness. And so, just as Lemuria may have been sunk in a deluge caused by the wrath of the Father above, so too Atlantis met its end in the volatile eructation of the Mother's fury.

To many people such mythological suppositions may sound

like pure fable and fantasy, but to the ancient inhabitants of Lemuria, who saw their God Maui raise up the North Island of New Zealand with a fishing pole, and whose wild Pele reeks havoc on mankind even today; and to the post-Atlantean, Olympian Greeks, who were ever ravaged by the wars between Zeus and his wife Hera, there would have been no doubt as to the likelihood of such a visible catastrophe being caused by invisible forces. The manifest is the outcome of the sublime.

It was no great surprise, then, for me to find myself split apart from my *soror*, who I had by then recognized was not only my partner in the soul's work, my lover, and mate, but was also my twin soul[14]- the other half of my whole being. And so in the months of her absence I was suffering the agony of oneness divided, on this broken island, the hollow remains of which might indeed symbolically represent the ancestral separation of cosmic forces which thankfully now are returning into One.

How do I know that she and I are twin souls? A reasonable question. Firstly, because of a number of dreams which both she and I had, expressing this very truth. That, in itself, should be sufficient proof, seeing as the subconscious often knows far more than the day-to-day conscious. However, because she and I had been brought together perhaps one incarnation earlier than was originally intended, we were also living out a chaotic mixture of karmic experiences, belonging to separate destinies, which often intermingled like two inharmonious frequencies, causing us no shortage of turbulence for some time. During one episode, when it appeared that we might have to go our separate ways- at a time when we were not yet certain of our twin soulship- I had a dream in which my father came to me and said that he would be with me the following Friday. And since the male aspect of God was represented symbolically in my dreams by my physical father,

---

[14] Twin souls are the manifested male and female counterparts which exist as one being on the sublime, invisible plane, and exist at the same time as separate individuals on the dualistic plane of matter. Twin souls are the same being, although that being appears to exist as separate and autonomous male and female aspects within our sentient, worldly realm. However, they are not autonomous, and, in fact, are so closely connected- like the two legs which support our one body- that whatever befalls one, naturally affects the other, even at great distances across the earth.

I believe, for many reasons, that my twin soul and I were brought together perhaps an incarnation earlier than would have been natural, in an effort to avert a tragedy from occurring to one, or both of us. Due to this we were thrown upon a four-year period in which the karmic inertia of our intended lives, for this incarnation, mixed with the now essential actuality of our coming together, and thus created a chaotic milieu in which we were living out actions pertaining to both destinies, the mixing of which was not always harmoniously achieved. Yet it was essential that we come together, and essential that we stay together, and essential that we complete certain karmic predestinations which had been set in motion when it was earlier planned that we would not be together. Luckily for us the living universe is malleable, adaptable, and conscious, or this process would have been like trying to act on two stages at one time- impossible.

this meant that God would be directing the show, without the least bit of doubt, that Friday.

Having not shared this dream with my *soror*, she and I went out for a morning coffee that Friday, during which I found myself wondering when God was going to show me what I was supposed to be shown. I was also feeling the urge to go to a used bookstore near the coffee shop, which is where my *soror* and I went soon afterward. However, during our coffee, my *soror* had drawn a quick sketch of a symbol she had seen in a dream, an evening or two before, which was basically two halves of a circle facing away from each other, representing wholeness divided:)(

Upon entering the bookstore she and I headed for different aisles, and, after skimming a few shelves of books, I soon found myself being pulled, over and over again, to one particular book on esoteric understandings. I kept picking it up, putting it down, walking away, then coming back to it, quite a few times, until finally I skimmed to the back of the book where there was a description of twin souls. I read the page, then put the book down without much thought, and walked over to my *soror*, who, I soon found out, was reading a book actually titled '*Twin Souls*',[15] and which contained, on the inside of its cover, the almost exact opposite version- albeit this time containing a man and a woman- of the diagram she had drawn during our coffee: ( ). Wholeness.

The Father was with us, and I knew then what the intent of the message was: we were twin souls, and should remain together, through thick and thin, as they say. For though the convergence of two different karmic tributaries had caused us great tribulation, the river was widening up ahead, and the torrent was heading for calm.[16]

---

[15] by Patricia Joudrey, and Maurie Pressman. Somerville House Publishing, Toronto, 1993.

[16] For the last number of years I have witnessed quite a few twin souls, many of whom, I expect, will not become mates or partners in this life. Why this is, I am not certain, though it must pertain to a certain readiness, need, or desire. I have seen twin souls who worked closely together, lived as roommates in the same house, and had brief but not lasting love affairs together, all the while never knowing that the other, right before them, was not other, but actually the essential half of their true wholeness.

Twin souls are often identifiable by their similar appearance, psychic dispositions, uncanny idiosyncrasies, and the spirit they exude.

I recall one time when I was on a ferry in British Columbia, and I suddenly had the thought go through my head of a very beautiful woman I had known a few years earlier. Minutes later I left the ferry, walked to a bus stop, and ran right into her exact male replica- her twin soul, whom she had never met, but who was the man whom, I was certain, was her other half. After chatting with him for a while I found out that he had lived in the same east Canadian city as she had grown up in, and where she was living even now. I also found out that a number of years earlier this man had been in a very bad motorcycle accident, had lost some of his memory, and had been recovering ever since. Then I recalled that the beautiful woman, whom I was certain was his twin soul- though

71

Anyway, many months before that calm came about, my twin soul and I had gone to Naxos- the nexus, the center, the place at which no imperfect wholeness could hope to survive, for the forces at the center are impossible to maintain if there be any cracks in the egg. The circle must be complete, or implosion or explosion is the inevitable result.

As I said, we had gone to Naxos, to write, to drink wine, and to make love, and instead, a month later, after our center had imploded, I was alone on a ferry, heading out to sea, away from her, away from love, away from wholeness.

It had to happen though, for, along with the karmic chaos mentioned earlier, there were also hidden, archaic divisions within us, divisions which still needed to bubble to the surface, be acknowledged, accounted for, and forgiven. For until all the cornerstones were properly placed perfectly beneath us, any structure we attempted to build between us would inalterably topple from its faulty foundation.

Our foundation had crumbled, and I was compelled to leave Naxos, and had decided, for no specific reason, to head for Santorini, though en route I made a brief stop on the Island of Ios.

It was early March, and the island was all but dead. I had planned to stay there a few days, but during the first night my Father came to me in a dream and said that he would be with me in the morning, which, I knew, meant that God would be fully directing the show that morning.

I awoke without expectation, but was instantly sensing that I should leave the island, for it had nothing to offer me. This, at least, is what I was thinking, though, to be sure, the important thing was not the reason for my leaving, but only that I left.

I have found that you cannot always, and perhaps rarely, be at peace when you follow the spirit, because to be only at peace would mean to not allow the spirit's goads of desire, curiosity, fear, boredom, discomfort, and so on, to be projected into you and so move you on to where the spirit wants or needs you to be.

---

they had never met, and probably would never meet in this lifetime- had, in a shocking turn-around, become a lesbian for a few years, and then turned heterosexual again. This was one more clue which leads me to believe that each twin soul inextricably effects the other, and what befalls one has great impact on the other, who is not other. For, with her 'male side' almost dead, and then as a weakened convalescent, it is no doubt to me that she, without knowing it, had to take on that male aspect on herself, and become the male of a female-female relationship for a while.

I sense that there are many such sublime causes which create the experiences we have in life, without us knowing that it is our invisible cords linking us to others- and, most specifically, to our twin soul- which bring about certain balancing characteristics within us, so as to keep the whole operational in the manifest.

72

Needless to say, within two hours I was on another ferry, now headed to Santorini. It was on that ship that I ran into another woman who belonged to my sister's spiritual archetype, and who was certainly the person I was intended to meet, on a boat I had no intention of boarding, that morning when God was directing the show.

I can say now that every time my *soror*, my twin soul- who was of my mother's spiritual archetype- and I were in trouble, an individual who was an aspect of my sister's spiritual archetype was there to catch me. This happened on three different occasions, on three different continents, under completely different circumstances, and so, although I cannot describe the sublime event perhaps any more understandably than what I have just said, I know that the pattern holds true, and that each stage of growth we are in, as our souls strive for wholeness, can be thought of as a ladder, the rungs of which are well described in the blueprint of the universe. If we take a step up, we receive the experience of that rung, and if we take a step down, we receive that corresponding experience, no matter where we are, or what we are doing in this life, for the sublime spirit is ever the operating reality, though the material mind rarely sees it as such.

I was soon alone again, however, as the woman whom I had met on the ferry from Ios to Santorini- my sister's spiritual archetype- had departed in a few days, so as to continue with her own travels, but not until we had each shared a great deal of our similar ideas and experiences, and had embraced the eternal connection between us. I stayed on in Santorini, writing, drinking, going mad with wonder, as per usual, and pining for the other half of my soul now across the ocean in Canada again, for though my twin soul and I had been seeking to elevate the entire cosmos with our love, our own union was imperfect, and thus our efforts had blown up in front of us.

And so we had parted geographically, but not emotionally, for the love between a man and a woman belongs to the very nature of the universe itself. The love between a man and a woman is the glue which binds the cosmos together; it is the bridge across the chasm of nothingness, the sanctuary amidst the apocalypse. Nay, the love between a man and a woman is Eden itself, the Garden, which is mirrored neither in the claustrophobic confines of the city, nor in the lonely lands of the wilderness. Love is a garden in which heaven and earth mingle, and in which grows all beauty, all sustenance, and all meaning.

For without love there is only the hot wind to walk forever into, and the barren earth to walk endlessly upon, while never finding peace, nor harmony, nor respite, because nothing on earth nor in the heavens can support a house divided, and only the violence of Christ, and the compassion of Mary remain to shield one from the neverending rains.

73

I was in the neverending rains, in the blood-red rain that ran Christ's passion onto the earth that Easter on Santorini. For the air had grown thick with the red dust of Egypt, blown across the sea for weeks on end, and when the rains finally came, and they did, and the Red Sea parted, and Moses walked out of Babylon that Easter on Santorini, the drops came plummeting down dyed in red and covered the white-washed houses of the island with the anguish of the division between heaven and earth, which Christ pulled back together, and holds together, eternally, on the axes of the cross.[17]

Later that Easter evening, after the lugubrious deluge had cleansed the earth with the blood of the lamb, I was invited to a Greek festivity, the end of Lent, a day like no other day for the Greeks- the day of their return to the flesh. For the Greeks do not renounce cigarettes, booze, chocolate, or swearing during Lent. They renounce meat. And when their forty days of wandering in the fleshless spirit are over, they return to earth, to the flesh, and feast like I have never seen people feast before- rapaciously, gratefully, joyfully, and communally.

At the festivity that night there were five goats and one pig roasting over spits, and the Greek men and women would tear outer chunks of meat off of the cooking beasts, and then hand these chunks to each other as if they were giving of the manna, and the recipients would eat as if they had never eaten before. They were eating of the flesh, returning to earth, and finding it good, finding it necessary, finding it holy. They were eating the body, and drinking the blood, and the sacrificial lamb- both the Son of God *and* Son of Man- held this world together like Hercules between two brazen bulls pulling in opposite directions, and the sky rained blood, God descended into the flesh, into the earth, and remains here in all of us, the Christ within, bound by separate chains, one to heaven, and one to earth, pulling together the spirit and the flesh, for Christ is the living logos of life returning love into the world from the word which is the verse of the universe, and is done out of choice, out of love, out of ecstasy from the union which creates this world.

*

three

This too shall pass. So goes that wonderful Hindu axiom, which, had I been aware of at the time, may have provided badly

---

[17] I thank my *soror* for this pertinent image of the actual event of the Christ.

needed succor during my regress. Regardless, things turn inevitably when the tide shifts, and as my energy waxed and waned in the smoke and mirrors of the day, I still went forth, found myself again, albeit without idea, without purpose, without glee, and yet plunged ahead some distance further, into and beyond myself, in the ruthless absolution of sublime, divine intent.

I had endured tests and received appeasements, but still there was no peace, and no return, only a fire flaming hot inside of me, inexorably engulfing everything in its path. I was its path.

After the resurrection of the flesh on Santorini, I boarded a three day ferry for Israel- that land where the spirit had dwelt in matter for perhaps it's most intimate and arduous episode. Upon arrival I immediately headed to Jerusalem, specifically Old Jerusalem, seat of the Father, the holy land.

There is no more fantastic, mundane, ironic, worldly, otherworldly, harmonious, inharmonious, and otherwise completely contradictory place on earth than Old Jerusalem. It is an impressive conglomeration of ancient Roman walls, early Christian churches, Islamic mosques, Jewish holy sites, Arab markets, cobbled alleyways, and trinket shops, all packed into a few square kilometers of humanity, history, and hunger. Hunger for salvation, hunger for power, hunger for money, and hunger for peace. The entire occidental drama, with all its passion and angst, collides here in the throbbing epicenter of Old Jerusalem, where a neverending parade of Orthodox Jews, Muslim merchants, Christian pilgrims, and an eclectic array of travelers from all over the world come seeking God, redemption, inebriation, or truth. Whether any of them find any of these whatsoever is a mystery to me. If I found anything it was inebriation: two parts ethanol, one part ethereal, which is a proper human martini.

The first thing I did upon arriving in the Old city- after checking in and setting up a mattress on the rooftop of the Petra hostel- was to walk the *via dolorosa* ...in reverse. This was a stroll partly intended, and partly not, for I had read about the *via dolorosa* a number of times, and had imagined it as a sacred path leading through a bucolic landscape, which would make for a pleasant walk and a unique historical pilgrimage as well. But in searching for the route, through the chaotic tangle of the labyrinthine Old city- which is not bucolic at all- I came upon the last station, Golgotha, first, and then, out of sheer pragmatism, retraced the entire pathway in reverse, to its origin, the first station of the cross, the betrayal. This act of heading up-stream, as it were, against the grain of history, was, as I said, unintended, though when I realized what I was doing, I was pleased. For though it is impossible to walk the world's most famous pathway in the opposite of the normal direction, without knowing it, I did not do this as an affront to Christ and his ardors along this way, but was yet glad to

75

symbolically scorn the agonizing, parroting, plagiaristic herd which walks this path now and every day. Enough, I say, of the crucifixion. Enough of the sorrow, loneliness, betrayal, and blood. The path Christ took ended two-thousand years ago, and He is no longer a dying God, not in my experience anyway.

I suppose that walk I took on my first day in the holy city was somewhat symbolic of my trip, which had very little to do with piety and alms, though I was certainly interested in the actual land the Man had once roamed free upon. I say free because, to me, Christ was the first libertarian man, for he was the most wild, most unkempt, most recalcitrant and most human *being* to have ever set foot upon this earth. And I wonder if it was the unrelenting freedom within him which terrified the others, who lived in cages of their own devising, and therefore they had to either destroy him or face themselves.

But I did not go to Jerusalem to alleviate such quandaries, nor did I go for a spiritual pilgrimage, because the only place to go for that is within, and no journey nor destination outwardly can get us there. In fact, during my time in the land of Cain, I found myself mostly hanging out with a couple of other lone wolves- a Danish and a South African man- both of whom had also left their mates, for one idiotic or perilous reason or another- and both of whom were therefore perfect unwholesome and ungrounded mirrors for the estrangement I was creating and feeling from my own lover at the time. Compared to these guys, however, I was like a tea-totaller and family man, as they were so far away from any type of unity in the flesh that only heaping doses of Vodka and Arak, the Arab liquor, could keep them functioning within their dull and relentless suffering.

The three of us were camped on the top of the Petra, a high point in the Old city, overlooking the whole vainglorious and groaning assemblage of zealous fanatics and penitent supplicants. I spent my daytime hours wandering alone through the catacombs and alleys of the many archeological and architectural sites in the area, hovering inwardly in a state of suspended awe and tension from walking the stone streets which were heavy with thousands of years of strife, struggle, and salvation.

In the evening I would return to the domicile and my brothers, and we would sit up on the rooftop overlooking the entire mad show, as darkness fell and a calm descended over the clangor, and we would remain there, putting back the beers, and soaking within the ensconcing mist of humanity's highest aspirations and lowest depravations.

To sit up there, in an ancient land filled with modern conflicts, and to have the loneliness of separation eating away at you within- burning a slow burn that does not scorch but devours you unknowingly, like coals smoldering through the roots of a forest, until the forest is dead and no one imagined that it was happening- is to experience what happens when you have wings but no roots.

Those were hard and beautiful nights, staring out across that thick knot of aggression and ideology, crammed into the ruins of an age long past.

From where we sat you could see the Western Wall, the Church of the Holy Sepulcher, the four quarters, the Temple of Solomon- the place at which he is said to have ascended into heaven- and the Dome of the Rock- the second holiest site, after the black rock in Mecca, of Islam.

It was toward this mosque that my Danish companion- who had lived in Israel, off and on, for over a decade- pointed one night and asked if I could see the 'black beam'. It took me a few moments to retrain my focus, but then I perceived what I could not understand, and what scientists have been making *ad hoc* hypotheses to explain ever since it was first recognized- a black beam, the consistency of light, but not light, in fact, its opposite- a beam of darkness, running from the golden pinnacle of the Dome of the Rock, up into the sky and disappearing into the very heavens themselves. Muslims claim this is their connection with God, with Allah, which seems to me as reasonable an explanation as any other. For the 'black beam' is a phenomenon beyond explanation, because, to the best of my knowledge, darkness cannot be projected; only light can be projected. But this was a beam of absolute darkness, blacker than the night, which is why it could be perceived only at night.

A very odd event, to be sure, and, to this day, it remains one of the most inexplicable peculiarities I have ever observed.

Let the physicists and materialists say what they will about such occurrences, for me the Old city of Jerusalem appeared as a confluence of many primeval streams, and the mysteries within and around it betrayed the profundity of such sublime convergences, whose turbulence creates and maintains the spirit's tangle in the realm of time. A tangle which I have come to fear, abhor, desire, and cherish.

Were life for me but a mere unobstructed vantage point, like the Haas Promenade, on the outskirts of Old Jerusalem, where one can see equally in both east and west directions, I would no doubt ease into the spacious gap where struggle and temptation are but spectacles of no import but to color the show. Yet life for me, and I expect all others, is no mere vantage point, and is instead an intimate exercise of an all-consuming penetration into and through what can never be grasped but only hallowed, cursed, or avoided. And perhaps this is why the darkness is as necessary as the light, why the flesh is as required as the spirit, and why love is as essential as indifference.

Indifference is the vantage point from which we choose the targets of our arrows of love, hate, or ambivalence. Looking down from that height of carelessness we see a wretched ghoul and pass over, and

77

then further on we see a tender child, to which we descend. Looking from the height of indifference we find the places where we will swoop down and enter with sword swinging, kisses flying, or boredom, or awe.

Without the vantage point the tangle is insurmountable. Though without love or anger in our hands, the tangle is but a knot of death. And so we need to be above, and we need to be of.

That we stand above, on a far-off hill before coming into life, and then, with a desperate mad plunge, take upon ourselves the ardors of this coat of flesh- which is no garment after all but an integral part of our true beings, and a part which we have returned to retrieve and claim as our own- it is only in this way that we can attain also to the transfiguration, the ascension, where the spirit and flesh are reunited and rise up together as one.

This concept of ascension[18] had been following me unbidden about for a couple of years at this point, mostly in the form of haphazard meetings with individuals who were, or had been, followers of various esoteric or new age teachings devoted to the attainment of ascension.

I believe that the complete liberation of the flesh- through its unity with the spirit- is not only possible, but inevitable. The confining qualities of dark matter have groaned under their own torpid gravity for too long already, and the lofty, rarefied air of the ungrounded heavens have concomitantly become cold and unliveable. The shift is coming. Avalon.[19]

---

[18] Ascension is a reality. It can occur when the individual has become finished, complete, and whole. In order to accomplish this, one must desire, intend, and will to become whole, and one must lose every concept of what type of journey might be required to get there, for everyone's path will be different. The flesh is transfigured as consciousness descends into and mates with feeling. Having said that, the work of ascension is the work of the spirit on earth. That means that one works toward ascension in a roundabout way- by healing themselves, and others, and the earth; one does not forsake this life, for this life is where the work *is*. Ascension will occur once one's earthly duties are complete and therefore it is a by-product of one's earthly existence. After all, what one finds in 'heaven', so to speak, is not much different from what is on earth. For what a person seeks to escape here will only have to be dealt with there, and so it is best to utilize this life, this forum, as the plane upon which one becomes whole.

[19] I believe that I have been close to ascending, like old Solomon, on two separate occasions- back when I was absolutely tired and full of contempt for this earthly drama, and wanted then, like I imagined no man had ever wanted before, to leave this plane for less limiting pastures, though my ascension did not come about, for a number of reasons.

At one point, when I was prepared and willing to go, Christ came to me in a dream and told me that I should stay, for reasons I do not feel compelled here to relate.

At another time, when I thought I had waited long enough, and was ready and willing again to mix the two elements of flesh and spirit and so to become the light which can rise up into the nether realm without dying, a voice came to me and said "All flesh is one flesh." And suddenly I understood the reality of what we are doing here, and that in each individual's efforts towards wholeness is the will of the entire earth and the hosts of

You see, only after the spirit has entered the mystic flesh, can the flesh escape to the spirit. Only after the Father enters the Mother, can the little flame be engulfed by the fire.

And this means that we do not truly enter the eternal realm until we truly enter the ephemeral, for that is when the type and archetype, the mythos and the mean, the Logos and the Son, are bound at the same diaphanous membrane between all that comes and goes, and all that never changes. That is when we become the emptiness within which all form exists, though first we must become the form within the emptiness, for stillness lies *within* being.

When we become the flesh completely, only then will the flesh become free. To enter into matter, to become matter, is to release the spirit trapped in matter, the Mater, the Mother, which is to know, to honour, and to become Her.

*

four

When you fall, as we all have fallen- from the stars, through the stratosphere, down the womb, out the canal, into the heart, and unto humanity, you are instantly captured, incarcerated, whipped, starved, indoctrinated, degraded and controlled. They get you quickly, and the horrors multiply unceasingly.

It's as if you are dropped into the sea, dragged helplessly under until you run out of breath, and only then do you begin to thrash with enough wild frenzy to break free. But even if you do break away, you still have to swim an incredible distance back to the surface, with nothing left in you but exhaustion and pain. It is desperate, to rise up with your body, from the bottom, without a breath to relieve you, nor a strong hand to tug you along.

This makes it much harder to fulfill our destinies. And yet fulfill them we must, for we have each been sent to this unique corner of the cosmos for a specific reason. And we must wake up, remember who we are, where we came from, and what odd and singular purpose originated the reason for us coming to this realm of matter and madness, to this world where people seem intent on keeping themselves in hell, a hell into which we then become accustomed, and do not consider leaving until most of us are so far immersed in the dark

---

heaven, seeking to merge all of our separated halves into a new and living whole, and raise the married creation to a freer height. Planetary ascension.

labyrinth that to then leave means a complete reversal of the direction we had been heading, which is to begin the long and lonely journey back to the beginning, to that place we had never really left but only forgotten, to our own sacred 'I'.

It's all about what we've got inside ourselves- what hunger, and longing, and rage built up from centuries of folly and separation- what passion we have to drive our selves through the walls of false understandings, irrelevant lies, useless facts, rules, and fears.

We must rise up every morning out of the ashes we each became in the lonely night before. We must rise up like ghosts from the death of unlove, into the impoverished world, and forge on another yard, or foot, or inch, whatever we've got left in ourselves. But we must, for our own sake and no other's. When the spirit has departed and the flesh remains intact, that is when the true work begins.

No longer do we grow peacefully upward like sublime lotuses, gently rising above the mud. Now is the day we must push our flesh up through mankind's hardened cement, and learn to blossom like mountain roses through the stone, with all our glorious, soft beauty, protected by our sharpened, merciless thorns.

And the only way I know to do that is to be yourself, to forgive yourself, to love yourself, and to forget yourself. To connect all the disparate layers of existence through the quicksilver of the self. Of the self. To be of. To return to God in the midst of things. To be the God-flesh of our own becoming. To deny nothing, to renounce nothing. To accept. To be of. To be.

There is no way home but to become home. There is no way back but to go forward. There is no way out but to go in. There is no way to become free but to forget everything we have ever been told, to start again, and to never look back from that road. We must dance again to the cosmic song, with the rapture of the lilies.

For society's comfort and monotony will only put us to sleep. Schools will teach us to turn away from beauty, and we will turn. Petty pursuits will unfill our infinite hollows. We will call it happiness when events conspire to distract us from the anguish of not knowing ourselves. Image will kill imagination, sight will blot the sky, thought will bind the heart, and we will live not laughing, and die without shedding tears.

And thus to fly free from such inertia will take everything we've got. Determination. That one word sums it up for me. Until I was determined to exalt, and love, and live my own life, I had no chance. And, to be sure, the day I decided it was time to leave my own hell, was the day the doors began unlocking ...of their own accord. For there is only one way out of hell, and that is the wish to leave, and that is all. But then, I also knew the costs. I knew that in a secret bliss to shame the gods I would walk life's empty streets as the loneliest person alive.

Lost and hungry I would fall in a cold rain weeping. The vultures of spirit would pick me clean of meat. Innocently I would come, undefeated I would go. I would exist without knowledge or meaning. I would be gentle and mad. The world would dwindle completely. *And I would live forever.*

*

five

I believe now that Christ called the Father down to earth, in his prayer- "Thy Kingdom Come..." - not as an affront to the Mother, but because Christ was already *with* the Mother, and therefore had no need to ask of Her in the Lord's Prayer, but only of He who was still and ever needed if the cosmic chaos was to be righted.

I believe this now, only after years of following the guidance of the Father, and dwelling upon the heart of the Mother. And nowhere have I dwelt upon Her with such intimacy, as I have in Hawaii, for it is there that She is alive, and conscious, and growing.

If Santorini is a remnant of Atlantis, then Hawaii is a remnant of its counterpart, Lemuria.

Upon landing in Oahu, on my first visit to Hawaii, I headed instantly north, out of Honolulu's fervor and moan, towards the famed North Shore, home to the world's most consistent and breathtaking surfing waves, including the ever impressive Bonsai pipeline. But I was not going there to surf- not in the ocean anyway. I was gliding instead on the sublime wave which the spirit sets behind one, so as to coax a person towards the distant shore.

On the commuter bus headed north I had poured over a map of the island and selected a Hawaiian holy site as the most proper locale in which to find a secret hideaway where I could camp unfettered upon the earth while trying to find some peace in the ethereal tumble. However, after disembarking from the bus at my chosen spot, I wandered about for an hour or so until I was fidgety and sensed that it was not the place for me to stop after all. So I hopped onto another bus and headed west along the north shore, until, just before entering the quaint little town of Haliewa, I noticed a large wooded area leading out to a beach, and decided that this was going to be the place for me to take refuge. I disembarked once again, and made my way towards the sea. En route I stopped to urinate at a public restroom, and there met a long-haired, middle-aged fellow who was punch drunk and alone, and was quick to offer me a can of beer- which, naturally, I accepted- and then another, and another, then a toot on a reefer, and so on, until we

81

were great comrades by the evening, and I was half-baked, and so I thought it best to find a place to lie down and dream off the buzz, at which point I gathered up my goods and thanked my new found buddy for his generosity and company, to which he unexpectedly recounted: "Don't thank me, thank Jesus."

Yes indeed, the wave of spirit had carried me across the dark sea of grosser possibilities and placed me on the implausible shore of a brother's soul.

After that first evening, I ended up spending a great part of the next week with Geoff, a dope-smoking, probationary, neurotic, beer-swilling, HIV positive, holy man. A holy man, I say, because he was neither respectable, nor did he have respect for others. He was a fool, a castaway, an ignoble scavenger who did not give a damn, and so he had transcended the oppressive bonds of respectability and sanity, and had become a fool in other people's eyes, a nobody in his own, and a fit vessel for the living, mad spirit in God's.

Not that he spouted any monumental, cosmic truths or had any great union with the absolute or anything, yet Geoff knew who he was, why his life had taken the turns it had, what the payment for his errors was, and how he was going to live, and laugh, and endure the sentence placed upon the remainder of his days. And that was- he was going to live life to its fullest each day, and not let up until he was harkened home.

I had met him very soon after the turn of the millennium, on my return from New Zealand, at a time when the whole world was standing a bit on edge, expecting that maybe we'd all be called at the same time. Perhaps this was part of the reason Geoff seemed at such peace within himself, because he believed that no one on earth lived without a sentence placed upon them which carried a finality as definite as his own.

Upon discussing the aforementioned millennial shift with Geoff, I remarked that it had not yielded the expected apocalypse, and then I made some flippant, rhetorical query as to why nothing had occurred, since everyone thought something would occur. In response to my statement Geoff, with an all-accepting countenance and tone, turned to me and stated matter-of-factly: "Because no one shall know the hour or the day of its coming", which is a trite, biblical misquote perhaps, but, after all, Geoff had been living ten years or more with his own, inner apocalypse, and he was certainly more of an expert on the matter of endings than most of the new age doomsayers who had been spouting calendar dates and predilections over the last few years, none of which came to pass, because no one shall know the hour or the day.

In Geoff's company I became quickly assimilated into a loosely-knit pack of homeless drunks, drifters, vagabonds, big-bearded pariahs, and pseudo-mystics, all of whom exist in substantial numbers throughout the Hawaiian islands, including Oahu's north shore, where these fringe types appear not unlike odd thistle bushes in a sea of roses, as they are mixed incongruously into the cornucopia of the bright and beautiful, fit and firm young men and women who have made this chunk of paradise their home. In fact, I have never been to another place on earth in which so many firm and fit, bikini clad vixens, and hard-bodied, rock-jawed studs abounded. It is no wonder that the television series *Baywatch*- known so well for its skimpily clad Aphrodites and Adonises- was filmed in the area.

Unfortunately for me I was neither interested in surfing waves, nor chasing dames at the time, as I was still strung painfully between two nooses, one leading to the spirit above, and one leading to the body- specifically my *soror's*- below. She and I were apart at this time as well, and I was stuck on Oahu, running amongst a pack of mongrels and misfits, and she was on Kauai, riding out her own tsunamis.

And so I did what I had always done every time I was alone, confused, impoverished, and free- I drank beer, smoked dope, surrendered, prayed, howled in bliss and agony, went mad with torment and ecstasy, slept upon the Mother Earth, beneath the Father Sky, met each morning balanced somewhere between torpor and awe, and left each day in search of the dream.

There is nothing left to do when nothing is left. You have to go on, without knowing why, or how, or where to. You have to find the force within yourself. You have to harvest the fruit that has grown within, thresh the chaff from the germ, and sew what seed remains into the pit of your guts, and hope that the next bloom comes bountiful, and soon. You have to plant that winter wheat in the darkest of your days, for if not, when the sun finally comes, you'll have no flour into which can be placed the leaven.

You have to find the fire inside, especially during the arctic night. And I hit that arctic night hard and brutally one miserable balmy evening on the north shore of Oahu, after knocking back a bellyful of beer and a couple of joints with one of the reprobates, until I passed out on the beach and awoke in the middle of the night to find my fanny pack, passport and wallet, gone. One of my brothers had gone sour, and my own inebriation had given him the open door to sin.

I was demoralized, because, with the loss of all the aforementioned paraphernalia, the last chance I had of meeting up with my *soror* on Kauai had now been snatched away from me, and all I could envision up ahead were endless days of panhandling, aluminum can collecting, paperwork filing, and the agony of loneliness, pennilessness, and loss. It was a cold and desperate feeling, to be without everything, especially love, identity, and money.

That was when I sewed the seed in winter.

It is said that the seven main islands in the Hawaiian

archipelago represent the seven main chakras of the body, and, depending on which island you are living on, or visiting, that particular chakra undergoes stimulation and awakening. Whether this is true or not I am not certain, and yet, having had the kundalini awakening on the Big Island, as described earlier, where the root chakra is the one being stimulated- which is the location where, it is said, the spinal serpent sleeps- I can at least say that this might be true. All is reflected through all.

Anyway, I was on Oahu, the throat chakra, the will, which is where the ability to express your desires into the manifest lies. Except the exact opposite to my desires had just happened, and I had no idea how I was going to right it.

The Judas who had taken my goods was camped well into the bush somewhere, so deep that he had bragged a few days earlier that no one had found him in the year or so that he had been there. And I knew that if I did not catch him with my identification and wallet on him, these would be scattered into the woods, never to be found, and no proof of his theft would be possible. I had to act, immediately. But how? It was pitch black out, I was in an unsober haze, had neither flashlight, nor idea where he was, and no thoughts on how to proceed.

And so I did what I have done many times, under similar circumstances of duress- I prayed.

As astounded as I am by the power of prayer, I am perhaps yet more astounded by how thoroughly disregarded this timeless method of communication is by the greater portion of humanity. Though I suppose the lack of interest in prayer comes down to a simple fact, which is this: prayers are always answered, but they are rarely answered in the way the petitioner desires. And by that I mean that what we ask for might not be what is best for us, and what is best for us might be far harder, or more sublime, than we are willing to accommodate. And a prayer we issue might bring assistance, but that assistance might have to come in the form of pain. And who on earth would pray for that kind of assistance? Who indeed?

Anyway, I prayed. I prayed for guidance, for assistance, for understanding, and for help. And in that receptive state which I entered into I began to commune with God, or my higher self, if you will, in such a way that I understood that this theft had happened because I had allowed myself to fall back into unhealthy debauchery to the point that only a small tragedy could turn me in the other direction. I then promised God that I would give up all the pollutants if He would assist me to regain my passport, wallet, and what little cash I still had.

Then, in that receptive state, I began to understand how, if I were to find the renegade in the forest, I was not to accuse him right off, for if he had dispensed with my goods he could easily deny it and nothing could be done. No, I was to say nothing, but let the vacuum of my silence draw out his confession, as silence often does, in front of which guilt stands very little chance of remaining hidden.

I was also subtly informed that I must not, in the end, have any anger towards the thief, but only forgiveness and love, because these are the only means with which to heal those so wounded that they lovelessly cause such grief to others.

After this communion, although I still felt uncertain about ever finding the delinquent's hiding spot within the thick acreage of bush, I suddenly felt a surge of determination, and of confidence, most likely sent down to me from on high, and I felt all of the sudden that I was no longer a victim of fate, but was instead a master of my own destiny, and I got up from the ground, and, just as dawn was slightly breaking, headed into the thicket.

I must have been guided, for there is no other way to explain what happened, because after walking for only a few minutes through the thick bush, and then standing absolutely still, I noticed a dim movement a ways off, which I expected must be my traitor. And so I walked slowly into the direction in which I had seen the movement, and as I got closer I could see a makeshift tent, which I soon quietly entered, to the thief's dismay, and then sat down slowly, and looked him gently in the eyes ...without a word.

We must have sat there for only half a minute or so when he reached to his side and disclosed my fanny pack, and then began a pathetic diatribe on how he had walked off with it unintentionally, because he had once owned a pack very similar. An absolute lie, but one which I did not accuse him of, nor of the theft, because I had been given too many lessons on clean living, prayer, silence, forgiveness, will, and love that night, and was so thankful to my heavenly guide that I could not have admonished this fellow even had I wanted to. And furthermore, I was really no better, as a few days later I broke my vow to the Father, and began consuming the substances I had promised never to partake of again. An action, which, I hope, has met with as much forgiveness as I had been directed to give another. For it is crimes like his and mine which are the outcome not of mortal sin, but of living rootlessly, of balancing along the unforgiving ridge between freedom and loneliness, a place where I found myself running when I no longer needed to run, suffering when I no longer needed to suffer, worrying when I no longer needed to worry, grasping when I should not have held on, judging when I should only have loved, and all the while struggling to end the war within me between the opposed combatants of the eternal instant of faith or of fear, and trying my best, while balancing between them, to teeter to the side of God.

*

six

Thankfully I believe that I was forgiven for my dastardly deception on Oahu, and for the rest of my ignoble ways, not only because of the Law of Forgiveness[20], but because I continued to be guided even after my transgression.

In fact, soon after that episode on Oahu, I did make it to Kauai, and into the awaiting arms of my lover.

And I see now that much of the division between she and I came about because we both had to learn how to be a couple, which is a different thing altogether than being two individuals. And, as per my part, just as Odysseus, who had to spend eight years on a peaceful island after completing his heroic journeys, so as to have the questing spirit domesticated in him, that he might return to Ithaca and be a caring husband to Penelope, so did the primitive wilderness within me have to be tempered and cultivated, until it became a Garden in which another soul could live.

And now it was on that garden isle of Kauai that my twin soul and I spent the next couple of weeks secretly camped in the forest, in behind a relatively little-used beach, where we rekindled the fire of passion and love which burned red hot between us regularly.

It is in and through this love union between a man and a woman that, I believe, we are wrenching back together the primordial duality which has caused the heavens and earth to be divided; for in the union of a couple's polarized souls, the universe, which is composed of opposed, involved, and dependent energies, is reunited in and through the love between a man and a woman, which brings about the orgasmic light of wholeness, of the spirit joining the flesh, and so binds the ancient fissure into the everlasting one.

And, to be sure, my twin soul and I entered without delay into the wild and harmonious, frantic and felicitous, shameless and lusting intercourse which caused the real energy to glow and grow around and through us, as it does with any couple making love like the Gods, and mating like wild beasts at the same time.

Never had I experienced nor imagined possible the erotic energy created in the living cauldron of our ever-changing sexual methods, perversions, positions, and possibilities. It is amazing how

---

[20] The law of forgiveness operates instantly amongst the brotherhood of mankind, uniting them against the hell of separation, but the law requires firstly the faculty of empathy to discern the requirement for forgiveness, secondly the strength of humility to ask for forgiveness, and finally the intent to live by the golden rule ever after.

many different movements, acrobatics, shifts, and thrusts two intertwined human bodies are capable of completing without losing the pelvic union. She and I conjoined intuitively, as if the complete tapestry of positions from the temple of Khajuraho were built naturally into our genetic code.

The passion that burned between us, and the friction we produced as our two halves of the whole commingled in the copulative benediction made holy in its uncontrolled, uninhibited, and sensuously pornographic delight would have been enough to light an entire city, had the energy been harnessable.

I state such things not only for the sake of telling it all like it is, but because I am a child of God, just like Christ. And I say this not as an attempt at comparison- for there is no comparison with the Man- but because I do not hold the image of Christ as an inhuman character, who came down to earth to castigate and admonish humanity for being what it is. I see Christ as absolutely, painfully, and courageously human. I see Christ as the essence of humanity in all of us, which includes our confusion, agony, inebriation, abandonment, philandering, and lust. I see Christ hungry for love, for sex, for orgasm, and ecstasy. And I see the guiltless bravado to which he gave himself in every act he ever did on earth.

I can see Christ insatiably slopping about in Magdalena's loins, shamelessly enjoying her honey pot, and then licking her slowly from her clitoris to her tits. Why would he not have done such? A man alone amongst men, bound to the earth as much to the sky- the Lord of the Dance- wild and broken open to the loss, the agony, and the rapture. Why would he not have given himself to the joy and mystery of the tantra of sex? A wine bibber, a glutton, and a rhapsodic lover, who dove down deep into the Earth Mother's womb, and into the open legs on Mary's welcoming bed. Son of a vision, mate of a whore, Bridegroom to God, Christ came to dance, to drink, to love, and so much more.

Let them call me a blasphemer, a heathen, a pagan, or lost. No matter. I see Christ full and purging all that belongs to and runs out of the flesh. I see him after a night of wild revelry, bent over on all fours, emitting vomit onto the dark stones of a cobbled alley. I see him spraying warm urine against a lone olive tree on a desert hilltop at twilight. I see him clearing his nose like a barbarian, onto his weathered sleeve. I see his shit curl in all-too-human coils as it exits his hairy rectum, and I see his cum launched euphorically out of his pendulous member and into Mary's welcoming caverns. I see it all for I do not deny Christ, nor the flesh, nor the earth, nor the heavens. I do not deny. I say this and a mad glee overcomes me. I do not deny.

I see Christ and Mary engaged in every act imaginable, from cunnilingus, to felatio, the sixty-nine, the wheelbarrow, spanking,

87

probing, petting, jerking, sucking, and screwing. I see it all, for I will not deny Jesus the pleasures of the flesh.

I see Christ standing naked in the warm wind, guzzling from a bottle of wine, while Mary is guzzling from him. I see him behind her, his teeth buried into the back of her neck, and his proboscis buried into her quiff.

I see Christ as a man without shame, without remorse, and without self-denial. And perhaps that is why they lynched him, because he exposed how pathetically everyone else had limited their lives through guilt and cowardice, and so his life was a spit in their face, a living mirror of disgust, and a fearless act of contempt.

For it was this same Christ who murdered me and who also saved me, this same Christ who demanded goodness of me and also demanded indifference, this same Christ who cared for me and also did not care, and this same Christ who spoke to me and who also was ever silent.

Christ was a man repulsed by the futile ways mankind deceived themselves and others, and he was none too slow to let others know this. I see in everything he did, and did not do, his belligerent, and determined words- "I will do as I please. I will eat meat if and when I want. I will drink wine if and when I choose. I will love Mary whenever and however I desire. I will work on the Sabbath if I please. And I will lie around as much as I can in the meantime. Take your rules, your lies, your judgments, shames, fears, and your deaths, you can have them, because I care for none of them."

I feel Christ's disgust burning holes in the hearts and egos of the citizens, belittling them, ostracizing them, and condemning them. And yet in his contempt and rejection of mankind's ways, I see his love, and hear him saying, "I love you enough to turn away from your stupidities, conventions, repressions, and fear, for in the simony of your souls do you sin against the God within you, and I will have none of it."

I see Christ in all the sordid ecstasies which humanity both desires and denies. I see him dancing a mad dance, because the world is not enough for him, and because God is too much, and the cup will not be removed but that he has drunk it dry. And so he is unleashed in a wild and euphoric, desperate dance of acceptance and abandon, a tortured and uncultured, ignoble and redemptive dance of the flesh, because he is here and now, the maker and breaker of mankind, a son of mankind, a created God, gripped in the feverish passion of one who has nothing, is nothing, knows nothing but that to be alive is a mystery and a miracle worth enduring through no matter what, no matter where, be it in the harsh confines of all the cities on earth, in the lone sorrow of the endless wilds, in the arms and hearts of his brothers, sisters, and enemies, in the rain and sun and snow, in the hunger, the satiation, the awe and tribulations, in all that it is to be a man, to be on earth, to live, and love, and take up your song and sing for the glory of creation, even unto the cross.

*

seven

From Kauai my *soror*- my twin soul- and I decided to fly to the Big Island of Hawaii. We awoke early, the morning of our flight, and decided to head straight to the airport to see if we could get on an earlier flight than the one for which we were scheduled. No doubt this eagerness was being inspired in us, because we did make an earlier flight, and only because of this did we meet, on the plane to the Big Island, a man who befriended us, and who, after my *soror* had left some weeks later, gave me a small hut in which to live, located near his house, on some land he was looking after in the Puna district. And then, due to my contact with this fellow, all the rest which was to follow played itself out.

What happened is that this fellow, Brendan, was in charge of a number of properties owned by a multimillionaire who was off island, for reasons I shall not go into here. One of the properties was a massive, pristine piece of paradise, containing a large banana patch, various fields, mango trees, and, most importantly, an extinct, forested volcano, inside which there was a magical little lake.

While my *soror* was still on the Big Island, Brendan took her and I to this unique property for a swim, at which point she instantly recognized the lake as one she had seen in a dream, days earlier, and was told in the dream that I was somehow connected to the lake, but she had not known, until we arrived for the swim, that the lake actually existed. This was a powerful portent, for after my *soror* had left Hawaii, a few weeks later, and I was staying in the hut which Brendan had offered me, near his house, I began to feel claustrophobic because Brendan was exhibiting a not-so honest approach to our friendship. And so I was thinking of leaving and finding other accommodations. But then one night I had a dream in which I saw the lake in a vision, and, among other things, knew that I was to stay where I was until things played themselves out.

Well, not two weeks later the man who was then caretaking the volcano and lake had to fly to Oahu for a couple of months, and, lo and behold, I became the caretaker of that magical piece of the Mother.

I say this with absolute candor, for though the entire earth is a part of Her body, there are some places in which She is so alive, so conscious, and so available, that to be in those places for any period of time, is to connect with Her so intimately that you feel as if you're sucking on her very teat.

I assume it was necessary that such a connection take place between myself and the Mother, which is why my *soror* and I had boarded the plane early from Kauai, which is why we met Brendan, which is why I stayed with him, and was told to stay, and not move, which is how I finally ended up living on, and loving the earth in a way that I could never have imagined.

To bond with the Mother in one of her hotspots is to hit upon an erogenous zone of the world, and to send sparks flying into yourself, and out into the cosmos; it is to send your connection with the Father down into the womb of the Mother, and to become the living act of coitus between them; it is to give yourself to the earth, as much as to the heavens, and in doing so to bring that Christ within you down from the cross, and back into the womb of Bethlehem.

I expect this type of connection is happening in many places around the world, though I doubt it is happening in any great manner any place where the earth is covered in cement and defiled instead of being deified. For, whereas the Father can be reached anywhere, at anytime, by anyone willing and earnest enough, the connection with the Mother is a more specific and demanding event; for, whereas the Father can be reached through the spirit, the Mother must be connected *in* the flesh. And so it is only in the unspoiled areas of the earth where She can be most easily embraced, interacted with, and adored. One such place is the Big Island of Hawaii, and, more specifically, the Puna district.

Puna is a vast area of natural beauty which is populated by an abundance of hippies, new-agers, drifters, back-to-landers, dope growers, mystics, maniacs, musicians, artisans, dropouts, ex-pats, saints, and infidels. It is Babylon. Though it is not the Babylon separated from the Godhead, but the new Babylon, re-united to the spirit and yet still anchored to the earth. *Terra firma, spiritus mundi.*

If the Big Island of Hawaii is the epicenter of the Mother Earth, with Mauna Kea and Mauna Loa soaring skyward as Her two bodacious fourteen-thousand-foot breasts, and the lava flow from Kilauea as Her ever-purging menses, then Puna is Her womb. And I am not being facetious.

Indeed She is as alive and accessible in the Puna district of the Big Island of Hawaii, as any other place on Her entire earth body. In fact, I find it no strange coincidence that on Mother's Day of 2002, the largest volcano in the world, Mauna Loa, began to swell, and at the same time Kilauea stepped up its lava output, as if to announce Her true being to the world.

It is in Puna where the orgasm of spirit and soul occurs, in

90

Puna where the Father's invisible member enters the warm womb of the visible earth, in Puna where the Mother cums, grows heavy with child, gives birth, and then suckles her children. Puna is the matriarchal stronghold. It is where the Hawaiian Goddess Pele calls the shots.

There are tales of large corporations attempting to create a foothold in the area, with the intention of building a resort and living off the fat of the land, as it were. But only tales remain. Each attempt at corporate or cosmopolitan insurrection has met with disaster, economic ruin, or a strategically placed magma flow, because this is one of the last places on the earth- which is Her body- where the Mother will not be fucked unwillingly.

Pele is known for Her fire, Her anger, and Her love, for She is wild and unbridleable. The offerings most often presented to Her by Hawaiians seeking Her favor are gin and cigarettes, for She is dark and reckless, always ready for a party, and always ready for a fight. Love and fire. To whom She loves She gives the bounty of the earth, to whom She hates She destroys.

There is a well known story told in Puna, of an old woman, said to have been a temporary manifestation of Pele, who wandered around the Kapoho area one day, in the 1960's, going from house to house and asking at each door for some food and shelter, and being turned away by all until finally being taken in by the lighthouse keeper. Rumor has it that she left his place a few hours later, peacefully, and gratefully, and the next day a lava flow wiped out the entire village- except for the lighthouse keeper's home. To this day you can see where the flow parted to go around his house, and then rejoined so as to leave none of Her compassionless children unpunished. Love and fire. She takes care of some, and wreaks havoc on others. And who can blame Her.

My own mother often said that if ever there was threat of harm to one of her children, she would turn into an unstoppable grizzly in order to rescue us, and I believe her. I believe that her love was so strong, that it could turn, when necessary, into a rage that no human could match. I believe this with all my soul, and as I write this I feel my body filling with shivers, and my eyes growing cloudy with tears, as if I can finally understand the love of a mother for her children.

And now I take this understanding of a mother's love, given to me by my physical mother, and I wish the same for Gaia, Mother Earth, whose children are in danger, just as She is in danger herself. For the earth is now all but a dumping ground onto which we cast our limitless garbage, and I, for one, will be glad on the day She declares "No more!"

No more. Enough is enough. I look forward to the day when the Mother's wrath, guided by the Father's vision, reclaims all that has been stolen from Her. And I believe this is possible, for She is not

91

unaware. In fact, it is well understood on the Big Island that Pele will not let lava be taken off of the island without severe consequences. And there are many tales of tourists scoffing brashly at such local warnings and deciding to fly home with a little chunk of the Mother, and then of these unbelieving heathens mailing the lava back to the island, a few months later, in an attempt to appease the force now ruining their lives.

Oh, She is a dark, ferocious, and unforgiving matriarch at times, this devouring female, Kali, Black Madonna, Green Tara, or Pele, call her what you will. She is your Mother, and She is vicious.

*

eight

There is a nude beach on the Big Island of Hawaii where the spirit runs as thick as magma, and all archetypes of the human drama are represented by those who are called to frequent this beautiful and secluded locale.

It is one of those rare places on earth which has not yet been quarantined nor corrupted by the ever fearful bourgeois rabble and their henchmen. It is a place where lawlessness gives way to freedom, nature gives way to nudity, and euphoria gives way to song. It is a place with aspects of Valhalla, Avalon, and Eden, all intermixed and resonant in the confluence. It is a place where a garment of flesh is the norm, drumming circles are regular occurrences, laughter and awe are the order of the day, and nature is the church within which the congregation holds communion.

It is a community of a handful of regulars, and a neverending succession of traveler's, transients, and tourists. And yet no matter what the mix of characters on any given day, the feeling is always the same: harmony.

I have seen almost every spiritual archetype- which I have come to recognize- make an appearance on this particular black-sand stage at one time or another, for it, like similarly chosen spots, is a spiritual vortex where God's own soup of souls is mixed to a particular taste on any given day.

It is also an area of incredible beauty, and oceanic delight, where I have had the privilege to snorkel naked with wild dolphins on a few occasions, an event which I can only compare to the float-flying feeling I have experienced in dreams, during periods in my life when my spirit lightened and drifted gently up and out of context.

To be out in the deep blue, warm-as-blood water, unclothed, and to be slowly meandering under the waves, in the weightless and timeless calm, amongst a graceful and carefree school of dolphins, is to return to a part of ourselves which is ever living just below the crashing surf of life, and agonizing to finally fly free.

The dolphins themselves must sense the calm on that uncommon beach, for they happen by it quite regularly, often lunging out of the waves in acrobatic somersaults and flips as if trying to express or release the explosive joy of simply being alive.

It is a joy which lives in all of us, but is so quickly obliterated by care and strife, though I believe this inherent mirth can be resurrected in a moment by anyone who up and tosses their oppressive worries aside.

As such, it was on that beach itself that I came to witness one person who carried that wild bliss closer to their heart than ever I have seen in another- a young girl, perhaps nine years old, who must have had angels dancing and smiling over her with delight at her uninhibited antics, exuberance, and authenticity.

Never have I seen another individual who lived so completely, so naturally, and so abundantly. Compared to her, the rest of the thoroughly alive and spirited cast on the beach were but walking cadavers, and lifeless puppets, for she was the living incarnation of Life itself.

She reminded me of a study I once read, in which some researchers had hidden a camera on the outskirts of a playground, to film children at play. The scholars were intending to do some such psychological or sociological report or another. But these academicians must have been far more lucid or inspired than is the norm, for they began recognizing certain patterns in the play, while they were reviewing the series of tapes taken of the children.

It was as if there was a sublime music running through the playground, and as if the tune would surge here, and then there- as if the playground itself was a living symphony, and the children were the instruments.

And then the researchers discovered something even more fantastic. It suddenly dawned upon them that one little girl was always in perfect harmony with the whole, as if she was in tune with the entire symphony, and that whatever she did, or wherever she went, the music went with her, or she went with it, for these two things were indistinguishable, because she had tapped naturally into the music of life which was being pulsed through the world, and specifically into that playground, and more specifically into her, and through her, and of her, because she was …Life. All others were merely instruments of the music which she incarnated.

And it was the same with the young girl on the nude beach, in that faraway corner of that fervent land, where I saw the living music of her being dance among the spirit's instruments, and in doing so she gave life back to the life she had been given.

Had I not learned by that point to empty myself out of all context and manifestation, thus attaining the non-reactive position of non-being, and the vantage point of present absence, I would never have seen this all going on, and so would not have recognized her harmonic expression of the whole. Luckily for me I was well acquainted with non-being, for that was my natural state, and it was only with the constricted corpulescence of being that I had to struggle towards and become, which is perhaps why that marvelous manifestation of spirited existence so powerfully enthused me- because she was unconstricted *being*.

A few months later, perhaps due to my intoxication with, and joy of, her spirit, or due to one of God's infinite unknowable plans, I was sent a dream in which that same young girl was saying something about wanting to go to the lava flow on the island. The next morning I awoke and headed to the beach, and ended up, unintentionally, planting myself right near where she had dropped her garments. When she returned for them she was speaking with some adults about wanting to go see the lava flow, a signal which prompted me to finally say hello to her- which I had not done in the past both for lack of genuine opportunity, and because I was shyly smitten with her, though not in the Lolita sense, but because I was smitten with life, and she was the most alive specimen I had ever encountered. And so we had a brief chat together- no doubt planned well in advance by the Great Choreographer- and connected our spirits through the eyes so as to never be apart whether we were ever to see each other again or not. Which we didn't.

Indeed, it is the pulse of life, and not the understanding which counts. It is how we wake, and walk, and hug each other.

For to truly 'be', is to be life's orgasm, to fertilize novel happenings onto the universe, which is the erotic intimacy of life begetting life, of mystery making mystery; it is to swell and be consumed by the infinity of possibilities, of the unendurable stimulations of new nowness, of the spasmodic, quivering ejaculations of life gyrating forward into what it is and never has been.

Life is this dynamic conception into manifold wombs, through which we burst forth uncontrollably, dizzy into moments creating moments, spending our seed about like a ubiquitous colander over the world. We are these orgasmic moments tossed and piled upon one another into a wriggling, insane heap of becoming.

We do not evaporate, we sizzle, burning hot and sudden, like comets breaking up into the atmosphere, feverishly dazzled by their own incineration. And so our lives become glorious sparks vanishing as quickly as they are born, and we are the fluid movements through forgotten experiences, purged so as to let other novelties appear, for we are created to continually create, and the only rule of the game is that there aren't any.

Any place but where we've already been, that is life's sole direction. To look back is to go back.

To be new is to be the ever-flowing never-knowing perpetual mystery of ourselves.

Like virgins deflowered in their first act, we are consummation, though release we shall never know, but instead only the blinding-forever-moment when the universe cums ...and we are its coming.

*

nine

The spirit manifests in groups, as much as in individuals; for just as lone atoms join to become a molecule, and molecules become material, and material creates the manifest, so to the individual is harnessed and fitted into a complex group so as to create a workable and unique molecule with which the spirit proceeds to evolve the universe. And, like the carbon atom- which is the base of all life on earth, because it can be bonded onto by so many other atoms, in many different ways, and can grow into great chains, therefore becoming the common matrix of all that is of this realm- so too, the spirit is bound and woven throughout the full breadth of the cosmos, and is the substratum upon which the entire drama builds and has meaning.

I was in Dharamsala, India, when this observation became crystal clear to me. I had come to the land of exiled Tibetans, and was living there for a month, reading, writing, drinking *chai*, and watching the dance of lightning play over the Dalai Lama's residence one evening in the middle of a week-long gathering of monks from all over the world. I expect the molecular conglomeration from their collective souls must have grounded the spirit in such a way that the electric ether could not help but strike that lightning rod of their united beings in a continuous display this one evening, for the display occurred nowhere in the valley except right above the monastery.

Though it was not that holy gathering, but instead another collection of individuals which, to a much greater extent, sparked my own passion and interest that week- another conglomeration of living human electrons that would end up providing some of my thoughts on the molecular workings of the spirit which I have just attempted to describe.

I had moved into a bed-bug-ridden hotel, built hanging on a

95

steep ridge on the outskirts of the town, and overlooking the splendid Himalayan valley. What struck me almost the instant I arrived at the hotel was how many of the residents seemed to know each other, and not just like travelers tend to know each other- for a night of impromptu revelry and balderdash, the morning after which a quick goodbye is said and then onto the next meeting somewhere else, with someone else- but in a real, heart-felt, familiar way.

Later that evening a fair number of these folks had gathered into the room beside mine, and I was serendipitously invited to join what would become one of the most memorable evenings of music, mayhem, and union I had ever been privileged to witness.

The air was filled that night for hours on end with song and harmony, as this group of rag-tag musicians masterfully jammed a holy litany of ballads, folk tunes, self-written songs, and spontaneous outbursts, as if they had been playing together for years, and had seemingly known each other for their entire lives. Either that, I thought, or they belonged to a commune of some sort, here in the valley. I could not see it any other way, for their music and souls melded and blended together in a union of love, talent, and siblinghood to such an overwhelming degree that, for the first time in my lone and wayward life, I wanted ...to belong. It was that magical of a gathering. I was certain that these truly authentic and marvelous characters were members of one type of spiritual organization or another- be it a Buddhist monastery, Hindu ashram, Christian church, or some other esoteric organization- though at that point it did not much matter to me for I was inspired and uplifted in their communal company, and knew very clearly, for the first time in my life, that whatever community of likeminded souls these people belonged to, I was going to join them ...the next day. That was how powerful was the gathering of freedom, unity, care, and carelessness that evening.

Late into the twilight hours the assembly dispersed, and I went to my room, lay down, fell asleep, and dreamed a dream in which I was told that the folks with whom I had just spent the night, and with whom I had fallen into awe and adoration towards, and was ready the next morning to beg entrance into their tribe- these folks had been gathered together to heal each other. And this had all been orchestrated sublimely, by that carbon molecule of the invisible realm, the spirit. I was impressed, to say the least. And, more importantly, I did not have to enter their cloister, because ...I already belonged. Not to this insular group, mind you. No, I was not a part of their molecule. I was a renegade atom, belonging to no specific molecule itself, but being received by all, joining all, and then leaving all. But now this did not matter, for I was a roaming piece of the cosmic whole, flung into the implausible bedlam of a limitless periodic table, created by an intelligence so powerful, so far beyond and ahead of our limited

96

conception, so grand and generous and conscious of each little lost atom, and capable of pulling together fragments from the furthest reaches of the globe, subtly congealing a marvelous molecule in a flee-bitten, filthy, traveler's hotel, and turning it into the House of God for a night, and willing the souls of all invited to grow in the sublime passion of the invisible world, that I bow down in my station, in my abilities, in my cares and concerns, for the Creator's glue runs into and through myself and all things, and the river collects its tributaries, and through the rapids, waves, and falls, we are all taken to the infinite sea.

But how do you describe it any more clearly when this type of experience and observation comes to you? All you can say is that, without any talent, itinerary, or ability of your own, you are always where you're supposed to be, always guided by thoughts given to you, ever meeting everyone you must meet who has been intentionally directed towards you, and that therefore all people are non-separated expressions of the Creator, that life is much grander and more directed than it is possible to imagine, that the actual is illusion, the illusion is actual, and God is now and everything. That's all you can say and then you stop trying, you live in the living moment of the emerging manifest, and ...you let *It* happen.

In this way everything in life- even the smallest, most trivial experience or action- is in reality a building block, carved by invisible masons, and placed in a way so as to precisely construct the house being built within ourselves.

For example, when I was in university, despite an inability to stay awake in class, I completed a degree in Biology, with a concentration in Ecology and Evolution, which I had chosen specifically because I was in love with the mystery of life. Ecology is based on the interdependence of all life, but little did I know at that point how absolute the rule truly is, and that every act and intent is a part of the whole, whether we know it or not. All flesh is one flesh.

Furthermore, during one of my insultingly tedious classes, we were required to do an independent study, and in going through the motions I stumbled upon James Lovelock's vanguard theory called *Gaia*- the Mother Earth- which basically hypothesizes that the earth is actually a living organism. Albeit his theory was actually anachronistic, and only vanguard to the patriarchal minds running rampant through academia ever since the institution's inception; Lovelock was merely unearthing, so to speak, what the Druids and Pagans had long known as an absolute truth- that the earth is alive.

Anyway, I did a study on Lovelock's theory, and was glad to have learned a bit of swallowable academia, and yet, because I was still thoroughly brainwashed, having been raised and deranged in the polarized dementia of such academic institutions, I did not realize back then that my affinity for the Mother was already growing within me,

97

even during those formative years of my conceptual incarceration.

In fact, as early as three years old, when I was caught going from door to door in our neighborhood, trying to sell the bums and boobs, cut from the nude bodies I had found in my father's Playboy Magazines, to any takers, I can see now that I was already infatuated with the Mother.

To be sure, there are hidden but living blueprints within the entire fabric of our journey through life, and not only our specific, individual life, but also within our connected existence, for the 'part' is so interdependent with the whole that the lines of division, distinguishing where one individual leaves off and where another begins, slowly dim and eventually fade away, as we dissolve from identity and infiltrate the whole. The connectedness *is* life, and the destination to which we are all headed is the same one, though our experiences of the trip, and of our arrival, may be very different.

My physical brother, for example, carries a very similar spirit, soul, and disposition to my own, and though our paths are as idiosyncratic as all others, there are also immense and deep similarities between us, for we are of the same fabric, and therefore are made from the same loom.

Knowing this, it was inspiring, but not shocking, to find that my brother had taken, while I was writing this work, employment on a privately owned, ocean-going vessel which, for a summer, was cruising the marvelous fiords and channels of British Columbia and the Alaskan panhandle, and was called, of all things, *Mi Gaea*- Mother Earth.

These are the types of occurrences which logical positivists call coincidence, materialists call chance, and the seers call destiny. No matter, enough of these types of synchronicities have occurred in my life for me to recognize, though not understand, a subterranean matrix, multifarious in its appearance, though arising from a common center, which we all can feel but perhaps never know.

It is this commonality, this integral core, which is each of our soul's brotherhood and sisterhood to all others. For just as a hive of bees or a nest of ants is called a 'superorganism', in biological terms, because the whole operates as if it were an actual being, and because no single ant nor bee can survive on its own for very long, for they are thoroughly interdependent with the entire hive or nest, so also are we not only mutually dependent on and with each other, but with the heavens and the earth as well, though we know it not, and so we pollute our brethren with judgment, our heavens with sin, and our earth with oil.

*

98

ten

As much as I have within me an East Indian yogini, an Irish monk, a Native American scout, a Teutonic barbarian, and a French decadent, so also do I contain a peaceless, wanderlusting Norseman. It cannot be otherwise, for I have been to most of the Viking Countries, including Norway, Sweden, Denmark, Scotland, and Iceland, and I can see no other reason why I have been drawn or guided to all such places.

Perhaps this accounts for a certain amount of my estrangement to the rest of the world, for I consider the Vikings to have been the original astronauts of the earth- the ones who would launch themselves into the unknown, to the ends of the earth, for no better reason than they could not keep still. In this way did those northern gypsies roam the harsh and unforgiving North Atlantic for more than a millennium, discovering North America no less than five-hundred years before Columbus- that southern European homebody- who, being not quite as nautically skilled as the Norsemen, landed a mere fifteen-thousand kilometers from his intended destination, and then proudly declared that he had reached ...India.

The Vikings, however, found what they were looking for- solitude. For the Norseman's soul is the soul of loneliness. Not a loneliness like the Celtic soul, which has been transformed and made beautiful and inviting through its music and poetic melancholy- but the loneliness of the north itself, of the rocks, reefs, icebergs, and seas which the Norse came to inhabit. The Norse soul is the most distant soul within the entire occidental family, though it is a soul which belongs to all of us, for we are all part Viking, barbarian, wanderer, and nomad, cold and peaceless and wild within.

I was sent to Iceland due to a series of four dreams. I did not understand what the first two dreams were trying to convey, but when the third one rolled around, I knew where I was being asked to go, though I knew not why. And so, for the first time in my dream-following life, I was indecisive, for I had never wanted to go to Iceland, and my funds were running short at the time, and perhaps I was not the best of spiritual servants the world has ever known. Finally, however, I recognized what I should have remembered all along- that the spirit knew far more than I knew and I was not to question but only to up and follow. So I accepted my orders, after which soon followed an affirming dream, and then, over the next couple of weeks I was informed, in night visions, of what boots would be best to wear, and what coat to take, and so on, for I had no idea what weather I was going to encounter wherever it was I was supposed to go when I got there.

I must not have been equipped well enough, however, for the morning I was to leave for Iceland I was given an old down-jacket by a chap in the hostel in London in which I was staying, an event which spurred me to suddenly remember another dream which I had somehow forgotten, in which I was with a man driving a large truck- the Greater Vehicle, as the dream symbology runs- who was worried that I would be cold. I expect that the jacket was His way of making sure I would not die shivering.

Anyway, heading out of London to Stansted airport that afternoon, from where I was to fly to Reykjavik, the bus I was on was slowed grievously due to road construction, and many passengers seemed doomed to miss their flights. I was sitting beside a peaceful, grey-haired woman who carried an air of dignity about her, and just after the driver announced the probability of further delays up ahead, I heard the woman quietly declare, "No, all of the workers have gone for tea, and the road will be clear." And I knew she was willing it to be so. A white witch, to be sure.

After we arrived at the airport, without encountering any further delays, and the passengers scampered off the bus gladly knowing they would catch their flights, I turned towards this elderly matron of the subtle arts, and whispered "Do you think any of them imagine that it was you?" to which she responded, "No, there are many unbelievers."

With that meeting as a send off I flew to Iceland and arrived on a mission for which, admittedly, to this day, I do not know specifically why I was sent, although I know that there must have been reasons. For in one of my dreams which spawned the trip, there appeared the message SOS, and soon after arriving in Iceland I was picked up while hitchhiking by a spritely young blond woman, and after getting into her car, taking off, and turning on some tunes, the song playing on her CD was SOS, by Abba, a name which in Aramaic means 'Father'- the one who sent me I don't know why, but He did, to that land which is the last vestige of that great northern race who worshiped Odin- the All Father.

Perhaps I was sent simply to meet this young daffodil in the north land, exchange a few words and connect our spirits through the eyes and that was enough. Which may also be the reason I was picked up hitching in the remote, north-eastern region, by the country's vice-president; an unprecedented event which could only happen to a long-haired, big-bearded, heavily-avoided vagabond on that isolated island of a mere two-hundred and fifty thousand people. And so he and I also exchanged words and connected our spirits through the eyes, and then parted without ever parting again.

Or perhaps I was sent for my own soul's sake- so that I might have a chance to walk upon and view the austere beauty of the Mother in Her unadorned and yet voluptuous state, for that is how one finds Her in Iceland. And it is only there, or lands like it, where fire and ice meet, and treeless, rolling green hills abound relentlessly, and an impermeable layer of cloud prevent Sol from casting His glare upon the land- it is only in places such as this that one must find different eyes to partake of the sublime, surreal, and yet supernatural abundance of the Mother.

In the austere, unforgiving landscape of Iceland, I found that I did not love the earth because of the trees, the birds, the warmth, or fruit, but that I loved the earth for itself. Because to camp in Iceland, in the barren, harsh, and windswept *living* land, is to find no fecund adornments wrapping the ground in swollen spectacle, but instead to stand or lay upon the bare earth, the unclothed Mother, and to suckle the beauty of Her being in a shivering, disquieting, intimate embrace.

It was in Iceland that I finally overcame my personal need to return again and again to the thriving, sustaining plenitude of the magnificent west coast Canadian wilderness, for I had now lain with the naked Mother in that northern land pregnant with Her supernatural spirit, and there I adored Her.

I say supernatural because Iceland is a vibrant region supporting the mythological world. Here one finds Mt. Hekla, under which it is said exists the theoretical gates of Hell. Here also is Mt. Snaefelsness, which was Jules Verne's inspiration for his story *Journey to the Center of the Earth*. And here one sees a netherworldly quality in the land, where mountains are not mere rocks but are the castles of elves, and hills are not simply inanimate bulges but are living mounds of the Mother.

Iceland, like Hawaii, is a land only recently tortured by the encroachment of mankind proper, for it did not receive its first humanoids until the tenth century AD, and this fact, more than anything, could explain why the Mother is still billowing with primordial delight there.

It is also a land still holding the spirits of its first inhabitants- the Irish monks, who came seeking even a more remote location than Stelig Michael for their otherworldly piety. And it contains the remnants of the Vikings with their Norse Gods, as well as a plethora of mythical creatures such as gnomes, faeries, elves, hobbits, and trolls, for these earth-spirits still find favor not only in the land but also in the minds of many Icelanders even today, and I can vouch for a strong sense of these nether-realm beings, whose dwellings lurk within the land, just on the other side of our realm, but continuous with it, and involved with it.

And so, perhaps I was sent to that North Atlantic land so as to visit a place which is suspected not only of being another possible location for the original site of Atlantis- the Father's creation- but may have also been a colonization of Lemuria, because of its unity with the Mother. And so Iceland is one of the rare places on earth where the

Father and Mother are each a substantial presence.

As stated earlier, He resides in the ancestral Norse spirits who worshiped Odin, the All Father, and in the Christian Monks who worshiped God the Father. And even to this day, the culture is so bound to that patriarchal polarity, that Iceland is the only place on earth, to my knowledge, that has a Phallological Museum- a museum of penises from species all over the world.

And yet the Mother is equally as strong in Iceland, for She resides in the living, gurgling land of fire and ice, and in the Tolkienesque remains of the realm of earth-spirits. And so the Mother and Father aspects of God exist together there, as dramatically as anywhere on earth, and they do so in a subtle harmony which might be capable of occurring only on such a remote island, battered constantly by rain and wind, hidden in perpetual fog, in a northern sea, which is yet a land warmed by the living blood of the volcanic earth, bubbling just inches beneath the surface.

*

eleven

Iceland is a land of lost witchcraft and wizardry, of sagas, battles, slaves, and seamen. And though I have often wondered why I had been guided to go there, what I had accomplished, what I had found, and what I had learned- queries which to this day I remain without concrete answers- I know that on that isolated rock, alone in the grey chill of an arctic day, I met again the Christ within us all, because, in many ways, Christ *is* the loneliness within us all.

This came about on an empty, magnificent, endless black-sand beach on the south coast, where I camped alone for a number of days near the end of my month-long stay. Staring out towards an empty sea, as I stared out towards the North Atlantic on that trip, is, I have found, a great way to wash away all but that Christ-loneliness within ourselves, and to enter into the self which hides within the self. In this way do we encounter not only our most intimate being, but we invert our vision, looking now inward rather than out, which helps the third eye open, because the third eye is spirit, not flesh, and so, by looking out to the unblemished sea, our sight can find no object on which to rest, and therefore all vision ceases to focus on 'things', and instead slowly changes direction, and looks towards home.

I have sat on many beaches in such a way, staring out to sea, and I have walked on many of those desolate beaches all around the world, in such isolated haunts as the Queen Charlotte Islands, the west coast of Vancouver Island, the Alaskan panhandle, the fabulous Wharariki beach on the south island of New Zealand, hidden beaches on Kauai and the Big Island of Hawaii, the endless shores of County Donegal, Ireland, and even the massive stretches of more accessible shores on Santorini, and Goa, in India, but never have I walked on one while as lonely and full of wonder as I was on the massive black-sand beach found on the south shore of Iceland, near the town of Vik.

This stretch of intertidal magnificence lies right near the main road which circumnavigates the island, and yet it is as remote as the seventh moon of Saturn, and is one of those few places where puffins and other sea birds, rarely seen from land, are as prominent as weeds.

And so I marched up and down that neverending beach for many days, wearing a winter coat and walking in bare feet, just so that I could be in contact and feel Her, and camping amidst the dunes, communing with the puffins, drinking warm Icelandic beer, eating cold Icelandic beans, and trying to come to terms with what I was always trying to come to terms with- myself, God, humanity, and the earth. What a maddening complexity of incompatible variables; take any one of them away and a perfect unity might prevail, but put them all together and all you get is a frantic jumble of incohesive forces and fields and a damn fine mess of the miracle. And perhaps this is the crux of the whole spectacular problem- that to *be*, means to be not only individual, but also in community, in God, and in the Earth, and perhaps we, as evolving beings, are not yet capable of perfecting this mad quaternity. And maybe it is this very unsolvable tangle which is symbolized by the four directions of the cross on which the Christ within all of us is alone and yet pulled in all directions by the inharmonious show.

No matter, if I was sent to that remote island for both love of the Mother, and also communion with the Son, perhaps it was for this latter reason that I was to meet a young man named Bjorn- a large yet timid twenty-five year old Icelandic musician- in a northern town, who, I recognized quickly, was wearing the same pants that I had seen in one of the seminal dreams driving me into that awkward pilgrimage. And, to be sure, Bjorn came forth with some interesting news soon after we became acquainted, in that he shamefacedly admitted to me that he often held audience with the Holy Spirit, and that *It* answered his questions. Yet he could not share this phenomenon with his countrymen because he feared their disbelief, their scorn and their ostracizing. To his confession I was quick to rejoin that perhaps he ought to rethink his silence, and, regardless of the perils to his ego and societal status, he should consider telling it all as it is, not only for his own sake, but for all others.

I understand Bjorn's conundrum, though, for it is not easy to expose yourself in a crowd of naysayers. And though Iceland held all

103

the pretense of a religious community, I was slowly finding out that, as a collective, the country had slowly fallen away from God, away from acceptance, and innocence, and into greed- a fact which would betray itself in numerous subtle events. For example, a number of times during my stay, waitresses did not give me the proper change back after I had paid, and it was always in *their* favor. And grocery stores often displayed one price near the product, but sneakily charged a higher fee at the cash register.

I was wondering if I was the only one seeing these subtle lies- because perhaps I was the only one paying concerted attention at the till, due to the pauper's budget I was on, and therefore could not help but become aware of the deceit being perpetrated throughout the breadth of the entire island. But then, as I was hitching towards Reykjavik during my last days on the island, I was picked up by an elderly fellow who confirmed my investigation, and who said that the entire country was thick with this type of deception, this type of greed, this type of disastrous, hidden, and cancerous unlove. SOS indeed.

This type of communal sin, which begets the coming communal chastening, reminds me of a conversation I had with another old gentleman I met on a ferry from Holyhead to Dublin, on my first visit to Ireland. After he and I had spoken for a while, and we had taken up the ever popular topic of the great famine, he turned calmly towards me and solemnly stated that though the whole affair had been disastrous and disheartening, some people believed that it was God who had caused the suffering, a point to which I agreed, because the spirit can quicken or chasten an entire group, as is necessary occasionally, which is why The Book of Revelation is filled with judgment for, or against, entire populations.

Oh, Lord, save them and every Gomorrah like them. And save me as well while you're at it. For I am a sinner who did not understand that true sin is simply a lack of love, and that this lack of love comes from judgment, which creates the duality of right and wrong, which creates good and evil, which creates separation, which creates death.

Luckily for me, somewhere amongst the confused trials of my erratic re-ascent, I met again the same snake who had taken me down, and again I bit into the apple given. But this time I took a bite only ...so as to spit it back into his disbelieving face. And then I said goodbye, and left him in his wily hell, and I walked back into the Garden to feed evermore upon naught but mystery, love, and the Tree of Life.

If only I had always known how easy it was to pry apart those bars of separativeness. To walk through, to breathe, to grin, to walk away. If only I would have kept playing in the play of the soul and nothing more- to be wrapped, in the rapt, welcoming, fabulous stream.

And though I am nobody and know nothing, I still come humbly to give aid to you who blunder on obliviously, with an offering to wash the mote out of your eye, so that with love you might weep the plank out of mine. For I have seen another possibility, another chance for freedom, as it were. And I will not go down without a fight. I have found the new garden in which grows no Tree of the Knowledge of Good and Evil, but only the Tree of Life. And perhaps when finally you become tired of the world and its criminal misconceptions, perhaps then you will seek to flee along with me.

I stand in earnest welcome for your tired eyes.

There are different answers these days. We must be kind and ruthless to ourselves. We must destroy the thoughts given to us, by abandoning every idea of right and wrong, and forgetting ourselves at every moment, so as to arrive at where we came from, and there to love without finishing.

And for this we must simply leap without descending, and climb without holding on, for there is no Way, no distance, no movement, no arrival, departure, longing, or fulfillment. Nothing need be done here; nothing to save, alter, deny, invent, desire, or understand. Nothing to seek, nothing to abandon. In the inevitable communion of our approaching new innocence, we shall reap not, and neither shall we sow.

Come into this new garden, come in, gather it all up, eat your fill. Here you shall find no exile.

*

twelve

Out in this world, in this incredible world, in this maddening, miraculous, mythical world, certain very absurd things kept happening to me, almost all of which I neither expected, intended, nor desired.

One such oddity began as another sequence of dreams, drawn out over a number of years, in which an old homosexual man was very interested in making love to me. I knew in the dreams that the man was God, which made me quite repulsed, and I always awoke with a sickly feeling, thinking that God was a demented old codger who ought to seek His fancies elsewhere. Little did I know, however, that this apparent homosexuality of God's was simply symbolizing the type of relationship He would like to have with me; He wanted to love me, but the only way for that to happen was for me to be completely open and receptive, and the only way for that to happen was for me to become as a woman in relationship to God, which meant to be concave to His convexity, as it were.

In fact, I understand now that a man does not become united to

105

God until he becomes God's wife, for to receive is to *be* female, and so to take upon the bridegroom is to become one with Him.

I cannot deny that this sounds like absolute balderdash. And yet, as always, a truth which I had refused to accept from within, had necessarily to present itself in the outer world so that I could accept that the spirit was not relenting in its project.

What happened is that I was in Ireland, and I was rootless and homeless, though I had never felt more rooted nor home, a paradox which could only exist in Ireland, because it is a land that has been uniquely made for blokes like me, for souls rapt in the wonder of existence and dancing madly without aim but for the love, the agony, and the brilliance of it all. I was dancing a mad dance inwardly as I outwardly toured the pubs of Galway. I was like a sailor who had never before set foot on land, like a man born out at sea, who had never known the feel of good old *terra firma*, nor of the type of solidity which belongs to no physical realm but is found only in the heart's vagabond provinces, and is a fluid perfection which the spirit knows as home. And if ever I felt like I had finally come to shore, and was home, it was in Galway, Ireland, for there is no place on earth which houses the lost and wandering soul in such multifarious pubs, like Galway. The town is thick with bohemians, hobos, troubadours, minstrels, mendicants, gypsies, hippies, publicans, drunks, and freaks.

I was staying in an anarchical, disgusting, congested, wonderful, and blessed hostel on the outskirts of town, wherein the most amazing cast of individuals were either living for months on end while working in town, or staying only for a brief period during their travels.

Anyways, before I lose the thread, it happened one evening, as I was sitting around the hostel's kitchen table, sipping on some cider, and bantering with a number of Europeans, that an Irish man, about my age, came stumbling in after a night of pubbing. He was blasted to the moon from drink, and he sat down with us and began spouting all sorts of nonsense, and yet he was in a somewhat lucid, dream-like state, and at one point he kept looking at me and declaring, "God is gay! God is gay!" to which I responded, "I know", though he didn't seem to understand that I had understood him, and kept on delivering his odd axiom, like a mantra risen from the drunken sea. But I understood him alright, and, not only that, I was thankful for his unexpected speech which supported my unconventional premise.

Given this corroboration, I can calmly declare that all men are women under God, though not in the sex and gender sense, but in the concave-convex sense; for in order to be intimate with God a person must allow God to penetrate them. And the only way to do that is to become hollow and receptive, which is a state of grace which I continue to imperfectly strive towards, for it is easier be in God, than to

106

let God be in me.

No matter, I was in Ireland, and Ireland was in me. And never have I been to a country where I was so quickly guided by the spirit, welcomed by the citizens, stimulated by song, and pickled in the pubs as I was in Ireland.

In fact, I ended up in that spirited hostel through a series of guided circumstances, as originally I arrived in Galway after spending two days travelling from the armpit of the world, London, and was weary and in desperate need of a pint of the black blood. So, upon arrival, I checked into the first boarding house I could find, which was right near the bus station, but I instantly realized that it was painfully clean, absurdly regimented, and as dead as the doorknobs within it, and I knew that I would not stay there long, though where I would end up I had no clue.

So I headed out onto the main, cobbled street, put back a few pints in a pub, and then went to a park by the river where I encountered an amazing assortment of young folks playing music, doing circus stunts, bantering about, and otherwise having a fine old time of it. I thought to myself- that is where the spirit is, in those people, and I stayed there for a while, imbibing their essence, and then left to get a bite to eat.

At the restaurant I was joined by a long-haired Italian fellow who was working at one of the local shops, and living in Galway for the summer, and who had some good advice on where to stay. He suggested to me another hostel, which had exceptionally cheap weekly rates, no rules, and no worries. And, I was to find out, after I had gone and checked it out, that it was the home of all those young folks whom I had been admiring, which was reason enough for me to drag my bags out of the soulless sepulchre I had placed them in earlier, and move into that house of spirit the next day, and that was where I met the bloke declaring that God was gay.

And though I am a man who enjoys his privacy and time alone, both of these were absolutely impossible in the tightly packed mayhem I soon found myself ensconced within, inside that broken-down, smoke-ridden, noisy, and congested rooming-house where the spirit ran as thick as molten gold: the Archview Hostel, or, archetype view, as I saw it. I was to stay there for two weeks, despite, and because of the human chaos within, and was to meet all sorts of fantastic characters exhibiting the maddest, liveliest, and most talented lives I have ever seen in any such wayfarer's community.

Every night in the crowded stairwell there would be guitar playing, song, and revelry. It was like living in a co-ed dorm in which no one had to go to class the next morning, no one had to study, and the only project was to live, and love, and spread the fever of euphoria around and through all who came to that effervescent stew.

107

There were a number of rooms in the hostel which had become known for housing groups of individuals from specific countries. There was a Spanish room, an Eastern European room, and a French room, which was the one I was lucky enough to get a bed in, for the French live life like no others on earth.

I had returned to my roots, had folded my wings, and found myself in a nest the likes of which I could never have imagined.

And so for the next couple of weeks, if I wasn't at the hostel, hanging out with those remarkable Europeans, I was out pubbing, to be sure. For Galway is not a town, it is a convention of pubs, albeit with a number of roads in between its various taps, an assortment of restaurants to feed the partiers, some hotels and a bus station to service the patrons, but these are merely collateral institutions facilitating the multitude of drinking holes in this one-of-a-kind west coast town.

I spent day after day patronizing the various establishments, listening to music sessions, and meeting the occasional local. One spirited fellow who beckoned me to sit down with him was putting back the pints as if he was inhaling oxygen, and all the while spouting gibberish about his 'master' in Asia, which was all very interesting, but I wasn't in Asia- I was in a pub, in Galway, Ireland, mad with music, joy, and drink- and so had little ear for his neophytic zeal. Luckily, however, he eventually switched channels and shared with me one important Irish commandment around drinking, which was to always leave the last sip of beer in your glass for the faeries. It sounded reasonable, although I was loath to give up even a drop of the juice. However, I capitulated to the local tradition. After all, I was consuming my fair share of the black blood called Guinness anyway, so much so that I soon found that if you drink enough of it- as if one could ever drink enough of that dark-mother's milk, but by 'enough' I mean no less than six to eight pints a day, a peasant's ration- your innards become coated with that dark and delicious tincture, and your stool becomes black as pitch. The first time I peered into the ivory throne after a few days in Galway and saw the ebony logs piled like cones of soft charcoal upon each other, I could not believe it. My shit was as black as the blackest night, and remained that way until I weaned myself onto a more holistic diet of cider, whiskey, and hash, which I was quickly trained to do while staying in that most quintessential of outcast's hostels on earth, and passing a bottle of the hard stuff around with groups of young Europeans, like only the Europeans do, and rolling big, conical reefers, like only the Europeans do, and taking in life, and food, and liberty, like only the Europeans do.

I had come to a place where I could be at peace, *and* in company, which is an almost impossible feat for a writer, because writing is generally the outcome of loneliness and quietude. But in Ireland I was able to somehow bridge the gap, and find a way of harnessing the wild beast but for an instant, not to quell its life, but to record it, and then onto the next stampede, and then a word, a sentence, a paragraph, some whiskey, a toot, a bit of laughter, some song. I had come to accept life in community, which I had never been able to accomplish in all my writing life, because to write, as I saw it, you needed to be absolutely alone, and absolutely still, unless you were a Maeterlinck, Nietzsche, Miller, or Artaud, all of whom were compelled from within by an overwhelming need to walk, and keep walking, at all costs, for only in walking could they find the rhythm in which they also could write. I suppose this is why Artaud went mad on Inishmore, an island off the coast of Galway, which is covered in a neverending labyrinth of perfectly square stone fences, the claustrophobic limitations of which must have oppressively harnessed that wild Pontiac and so brought him to destruction, for when a man with no wings searches the earth for a place to soar, his search is in vain, for life on earth is not about soaring above, but about lifting that which is below, because the roots must always take hold in the writhing, primeval soup, and only wings strong enough to remain tethered to those roots, and yet rise upward like a kite on a string can secure the soul in the tumbling tide. For just as the soul is anchored on earth, so must the spirit be anchored above, for each is dependent on the other. It is this dynamic- of the spirit rooted in the heavens, and the soul rooted upon the earth- which demands our strong flight into the gales above, simply to still the soul below in the smashing, manifest sea without breaking the line between the soil and the sky, for only then is the union of heaven and earth ever won. This is the tension of the Christ holding onto both the soul in the sea, and the spirit in the sky, and never releasing one for the other. For we must belong to both Heaven and Earth, to the Father and the Mother, to the Spirit and the Soul, if we are to bridge the gulf which destroys us.

We must become a flowing which flows as matter flows, like one gigantic sea which swells and thunders here and there, is calm and inviting elsewhere, and yet is always but one sea not divided but for the mind which says it is so.

*

thirteen

I certainly drank my fair share of Guinness during my stay in Ireland, though my intake was nothing compared to that of a brilliant young cossack named Jim Gains, whom I met in a country hostel, just outside the town of Donegal. Jim was on a year-long drinking binge, which began soon after his younger brother died in his arms in the aftermath of a head-on automobile collision, the trauma of which had led Jim to the pub- any pub- everyday for the last year, from 10:00 am in the morning until the publican poured him out onto the street in the wee hours. Jim was as hard at the sauce as they come, and boy was he all the more pugnacious, perspicacious, and laughably entertaining because of it, for though he was thickly embalmed with the booze, it seemed he was born for it- like many a Celtic man- and would live his life out and attain a ripe old age despite the chronic pickling- or perhaps because of it.

Jim was as crazy as they come, and full of euphoria for life. He related to me how one night, while visiting Paris, he and some friends snuck into the well-guarded cemetery containing Jim Morrison's grave, and poured an entire bottle of Jack Daniel's over the tombstone, in veneration and respect, and then cracked another bottle and downed it between the group, before laying down and sleeping that night by the tomb.

I spent a day wandering around Donegal Town with Gains, sipping cider near the ocean, and sharing stories, poems, and ribaldry. He was a fine mate to endure the world with at that time, although I was noticing that he was so full of wild energy, so full of his own effect on others, and so full of making merry from whatever came to him, that he was off his center, and I had the sense that something was going to collapse around him, which did.

As we were walking back to the hostel, which was on the outskirts of Donegal Town, we passed some travellers headed the other way. These folks had just found a baby kitten in the forest, but were soon to be boarding a bus, and so asked if we would take the cat and try to find a home for it. As I was by then refusing to get tangled in other people's lives, karma, and creations, I had no intention of taking the kitten, but Jim immediately jumped at the possibility, without much thought, and soon we were headed back to the hostel again, he with a pussy in his paws.

After arriving, Jim asked anyone and everyone if they would be interested in taking the little kitten as a pet, which none of them were. And so it quickly dawned on him that he had taken upon himself a responsibility which he had no desire to fulfil, and now he was the owner of a feeble little animal, whom no one else wanted, and neither could he keep, for he was soon leaving town as well, and there was no way he could be a pet owner, not with his unpredictable and untethered lifestyle anyway. He soon became morose, anxious, and a bit unstrung, as his life was now in shambles, because he had thoughtlessly embraced a possibility simply because it was a possibility, and he had taken on someone else's burden without realizing what that meant.

In very short time he was such a wreck that he was talking

110

about clubbing the cat over the head, because he could not take it with him, and no one else wanted it, and it was going to have a horrid time if he simply abandoned it, so he might as well end its life before the suffering began.

At the height of his frenzy he and I were sitting out on the front lawn of the hostel, and he turned to me and, with a desperate tone to his voice, asked, somewhat rhetorically, "I wonder what Christ would do in a situation like this?", a question which I have often asked myself, so often in fact that I have actually come up with an answer: he would pray, for that is what Christ did when there was nothing left to do, because he knew that he could do nothing of his own power. And so I related this to Jim, who, though he was a strongly spiritual man, thought maybe I was playing with him, because what can prayer do at a time like this?

Well, Jim's conundrum and confusion continued, and we sat out there for another hour or so, and the tempest within him surged on, until once again he turned to me and asked, "What would Christ do?", to which I rejoined, this time emphatically, "Christ would pray!"

I could see the wheels now churning within Jim's overwrought cranium, and with a last look of capitulation he got up and ran into the hostel, and I knew he was going in to pray.

Jim had gone upstairs, found himself a quiet, empty room, and laid his soul bare in front of God. And when he came back downstairs the proprietress of the hostel told him that she had decided to take the cat.

Jim was elated, and not only that, he had experienced what the most powerful powerless man to ever walk upon the tempestuous shores of this psychic realm had known full well- "Of myself I can do nothing", and so he prayed.

*

fourteen

After my encounter with the notorious Jim Gains, I headed to the northern coast of County Donegal, and if I have said that Ireland is as close to home as I have ever felt, then it was on those massive deserted beaches in the far north of the country that I found my bedroom. After all, the word 'Donegal', in old Gaelic, means- Fortress of the Foreigner. A perfect place for me to belong while not-belonging.

I had been informed by another traveller of a magical little hostel near Dunfanaghy, and I arrived there one afternoon to find that it was run by a trinity of marvellous folks- a French woman, a Dutch woman, and an Irish fellow. The Irish bloke was so spritelike that he could have just been lifted out of the Hobbit Shire. His name was Fergal, which means: man of gold. The true gold. And boy did I take a liking to him, and vice versa. We shared many a pint between us, sitting around the peat fire, or out in the magical moors of that remote region.

The hostel had been built out of an old grain mill, which had been built over an ancient Celtic power spot. The owner was a brilliant, ex-military man, who said he had been guided to buy the property, and restore the mill, but that was all he knew, except ...that magic happened there. And, to be sure, it is one of only two places I can recall at this time in which, the moment upon entering, I felt the spirit surging through every stone, beam, and adornment.

As well, the estate was endowed with a small creek, some fields, a few hillocks, and a little grotto where you could go and sit and become one again with the land of faeries.

During my stay at the hostel I became well acquainted with the folks who were running the place, as well as a few patrons, and one long summer afternoon we held a beach party on one of the endless coastal beaches which are a plenty in that area.

I have had my day of drunken revelry, and I have had my share of wild and reckless gatherings, but for some reason I will always remember that afternoon and evening as one of the most remarkable events in my life.

I suppose, if I can put this last statement into perspective, I say such because I encountered on that beach a juxtaposition which I had always lived with but which in the past had eaten away at me, rather than elating me. And that juxtaposition was this: I found during the many hours that our gathering of kindred souls spent on that outer shore, which ran well into the middle of the night, that I had suddenly merged the two necessities of my being, without intending to do so, but somehow it had happened, as if by providence; for I was now out on a remote, spectacular, and forgotten coast, as I have always loved to be, but I was also with my tribe, and so I had finally reached a metaphysical union of opposites, wherein I was hovering in the realm of lostness *and* foundness, of not-belonging *and* belonging, of loneliness *and* companionship, of distance *and* of intimacy.

To be out there, on the wild side of life, far from the clamour and groan of the world, and yet to be a member of an inclusive clan, none of whom belonged anywhere, but all of whom belonged there that evening, a motley crew of homeless drifters, on the outer edge of the earth, in rapture and aloneness, in sorrow and company, together in separation, one night, one wild, windy, manic, drunken night in which to revel, to sing, to dance, and to drink, because we had finally found communion and togetherness, and had suddenly become a part of the universe in its lonely, undivided, and ecstatic mystery.

It was the remoteness married to the intimacy, and the alienship married to the sense of home, which drove me mad with a feeling of joy married to melancholy, the union of which is the absolute make-up of the soul. I was in the world, and of the world, and not-of the world.

The feeling that this gave me ignited the remembrance of another beach such as the one we were on that night- back when I was on Oahu, years before, alone and without comrades, and I lay down on my back, in the blackest of nights, and looked out into the infinite cosmos, and for the first time in my life I began to have a sensation of earthly vertigo, because I began to feel that I was in the space which I was looking at. Which is to say, I suddenly realized that when I looked into outer space, that I was *in* outer space- and I knew, with categorical lucidity, that no matter what else we are- and I expect we are many things- we are also aliens, somehow living now on this forgotten planet, with forgotten people, singing forgotten songs.

And perhaps it was because of that experience on Oahu, that now I had finally found the peace and joy on the beach in Donegal, which was the fruit of that seed of foreignness planted years earlier on Oahu.

And it is this recognition which allows me now to declare that I believe we come from the earth, *and* from the stars, and it is only in the union of these two aspects of ourselves- the juxtaposition of belonging and not-belonging- that we become cosmically whole.

I see now that I belong on this earth as much as any man. And I belong in the sky as well.

I expect this is the case for all of us- that because we come from both the earth and the sky, we find no peace in between them. And therefore it is up to us to find a way to belong, not to one or the other, but to both. For we come from an infinity which we shall forever darkly remember, and though its recollection sinks down into the darkest depths of this earth, the dull remembrance will haunt us all our days unless we finally come to terms with who and what we are. For it is out from the infinity of Self that we have landed in the finitude of this world, and though we must honor, love, and cherish the privilege of our stay, we must never forget that our seed also comes from another place beyond the Milky Way.

*

113

PART III:
THE FATHER, THE SON,
AND THE MOTHER

*"...for it is our task to imprint this provisional, perishable earth so deeply, so patiently and passionately in ourselves that its reality shall arise in us again 'invisibly'. ...The earth has no way out other than to become invisible: **in** us who with part of our natures partake of the invisible...and can increase our holdings in the visible during our sojourn here ...We are the transformers of the earth... ."*
Rainer Maria Rilke

"The cosmos consists of the Father, Son, and Matter, each of which three principles contains many forces. Midway between the Father and Matter, the Son, the Logos, has his place, the Serpent that moves eternally toward the unmoved Father and moved Matter; now it turns to the Father and gathers up forces in its countenance; and now, after receiving the forces, it turns toward matter, and upon Matter, which is without attribute and form, the Son imprints the ideas that had previously been imprinted upon the Son by the Father. Moreover, no one can be saved and rise up again without the Son, who is the serpent. For it is he who brought the paternal models down from aloft, and it is he who carries back up again those who have been awakened from sleep and have resumed the features of the Father."
Hyppolytus

114

one

A few years ago any talk of aliens- and by that I mean visitors from other planets or realms- would have meant very little to me, except as a possibility which I had not discarded, nor yet accepted within myself. But a sequence of unexpected incidents brought the alien concept into closer proximity to my own life.

This began slowly and innocently enough, with a series of synchronicities- which is always a good sign that the greater consciousness is at work within the part- during my stay in Iceland. While I was there I had found myself reading passages out of a number of books describing alien encounters and abductions. The books were interesting enough, but I gave them little thought until I was sitting in the Reykjavik airport while waiting to fly back to England, and an Icelandic gentleman about a decade older than myself sat down beside me and instantly began an extended soliloquy on various enigmas, occult happenings, and alien encounters, which he described in a very similar manner to what I had been reading a few days earlier.

After our brief chat I boarded the plane, landed in London, and had a full day to idle about while waiting for an overnight bus to Scotland, where I was planning to meet up with my *soror*. Since London is one of my most hated places on earth, I did the only thing I could think of in order to survive the day- I bought a bag full of beer, and headed to the most remote corner of Hyde Park I could find, although remote is an audacious misnomer in this case, for there is nowhere to hide in London, no serenity, no peace, no respite, only the ongoing movement and hum of maniacs, motors, monarchy, and misanthropes. The hub of the British Empire. A sewer. A cultureless, lifeless scab upon the earth. Like all cities, only worse.

On my way to the park I picked up a free entertainment guide from a street vendor, because I noticed there was an article on Kurt Cobain within it, and I was morbidly curious as to why people such as he take their own lives, which is something I have never been able to comprehend, because life is such a marvellous, inexplicable, profound gift, and I cannot understand why people do away with it. Suicide astounds and bewilders me.

I recall reading that the Buddha once said that to be born on this earth is as improbable as finding one needle on the highest mountain, and then finding another needle in the deepest ocean. And so I wonder- why can't people see this? Why all the rushing about? Why all the petty agonies, mundane conceptions, and useless distractions? Why the trepidation? Why the anger? Why the pathos? Oh, to be sure, at times in my life I have possessed all of these imbecilities, but never have I thought of ending this marvellous benediction, for though I

115

recognize how discomforting it is to live on this amazing earth, in this incomprehensible life, amongst an abundant realm which could arguably be the most magnificent place in the universe, and yet still find oneself battling the ever ensuing flood of ennui, despair, discontent, and want, I still maintain it is well worth it. And I mean it when I say that I cannot fathom why we are impoverished within the beauty, tormented within the rapture, corrupted amongst the glory, and lonely in the Presence. I do not know, and can explain this neither to myself, nor another- why the awe and the gratitude go hand in hand with the disgust and contempt I have no clue, though thankfully I am at least aware enough to accept that the miracle and the mystery within and all about me is worth every penny of the price, for I have walked that bridge between ecstasy and ardor my whole life, and cannot deny its reality. And perhaps this is the last duality I must confront, embrace, and be done with. For perhaps I am not yet at the orgiastic center from which all opposites arise, and I must still face the ultimate release of both acceptance and rejection, desire and repulsion, discontent and joy, and perhaps only in those dual abandonments shall I finally rise beyond the cosmic tensions, and become the living One.

Anyway, I sat down under a tree in Hyde Park- where there is no place to hide- surreptitiously cracked open a can, and began to read the entertainment tabloid I had found, though I went slowly, and had read only a few pages before falling to sleep under the polluted sun, having quickly polished off a few cans of the juice. However, during that sleep I kept dreaming that I was still reading the article about Cobain, and that I was recognizing something familiar in it, the tone of voice or something, which made me, upon reawakening, assume that maybe I was being told to continue reading it. And no doubt I was, because soon after carrying on with the article I read that Cobain had once made a short movie in which he attempted to prove to his family that aliens had landed in their back yard. The article stated that Cobain also claimed, as a young man, that when he had become famous he would blow his head off, which sounded like he was a pre-programmed being or something. This fact, and a few other similar points in the article led me to accept that I was definitely being directed to certain information.

Later that day I boarded a night bus headed for Scotland, met up with my lover the next morning, quickly bagged her, and was bagged by her, in the usual way that we bagged each other after we had been apart for a spell, and then, after rebalancing our intimate polarities through the euphoric exchange of bodily fluids, we headed for the mystical Avalon-like isles off the northern tip of Scotland- the Orkneys.

The Orkney Islands are an amazing little archipelago in the North Sea, and not only for their natural beauty, but also because they contain two of the most quaint towns I have ever been in, excluding, of course, remote Himalayan mountain villages with no road access. Stromness is a magnificent stone village, where one feels as if they had returned to the Middle Ages, and a public hanging will be happening at noon. And Kirkwall, although less inviting in its rustic splendor, has the luxury of containing the millennium old, and disturbingly uplifting St. Magnus cathedral. It was in this holy temple where I took communion for only the second time in my life, and where I was staggered to find that the community of this church had somehow managed to utilize the nicest Port I have ever tasted, as the blood.

It was also in these two ancient and charmed villages, in this land rich in archaeological ruins, stone circles, sea birds, old buildings, and fertile farmland that, during our stay, my mate and I found ourselves, on two separate occasions, making a spontaneous change of plans, turning around on our heels, and then, almost instantly, meeting up with one of the very eccentric islanders, who, in very short order, brought up, of their own accord, stories of alien encounters, abductions, and how humans are to aliens as cows are to humans.

The synchronicities had piled up to a critical mass, and it was not long after this that I began awakening in the middle of the night totally paralyzed- like all the stories of abductions describe- and witnessing little beings escaping from my view. The paralysis was quick to wear off, but the encounters continued occurring every few days for the next couple of months, and I was beginning to wonder what sort of jeopardy I might be in, and worrying about what was going on while I was asleep during the visitations. Luckily I am not one to take such things lying down, so to speak, and after a few more incidences I decided that there was not enough communication from the aliens to warrant my allowing them to tamper with my being anymore, for, after all, it was *my* being, and so finally one night I awoke in the midst of my own violent outburst against the intruders at which point they vanished, and bothered me no longer.

All this may come off as a load of hallucinatory mumbo-jumbo, and perhaps that is all it is. I make no claims about anything. I am a man who knows nothing, a fact to which I openly admit. And I accept that the 'alien' visitations could have been purely psychological constructs of mine, or, of the greater Self, which is a reasonable assumption, since the last little man to visit me had a shaggy mane of hair, not unlike myself at the time- though he himself was only about three feet high- and may therefore have been either a psychological production from my unconscious, or a certain aspect of myself, finally breaking into this plane through the veil from an alter realm.[21]

And so I cannot truly say now whether I was actually visited

---

[21] An interesting addendum to this is that Christ was called 'Allogenes', in the *Nag Hammadi Library*, a name which means- alien.

by aliens, or whether all that occurred was instead the creative production of my own Godself, leading me down a tunnel so as to keep me distracted and avoid my figuring out the true game. I do know, however, that since experiencing those alien episodes, I have had a number of individuals confess to me, out of the blue, that they have had experiences which can most easily be explained as alien encounters. I have also had astral connection with two close friends, and in that alter dimension have seen their 'alien' selves, which are not apparent in this realm. And I have received certain messages that aliens are real, and, for the most part, well hidden.

This is a difficult topic to discuss, though, for the Godself is ever at play, ever creating new and more complex obstacles, challenges, and realities so as to keep the self bound into the show, while the Godself lays back and enjoys it. Were it not for the fact that one, and only one, event is occurring, it would be easy to retreat into multiplicity, and its infinite dramas, to explain the happenings of life. But that the alien episodes came and went for me, leads me to believe that I was only being tested by my Godself, who hung a carrot out in front of the self, to see if I would bite. Luckily I am no jackass- except, of course, to a curious Muslim boy on a puffing diesel rocket ship bound for a terrestrial, yet alien land, in this infinite, outlandish, excruciating life.

Oh, indeed, this is a realm of mystery, a world of miracle, and a life of awe. And the Self that creates it does so for reasons I cannot fathom, for I am the Self that creates what I cannot fathom.

And thus, I throw my hands up in bewilderment and gratitude, because I can find no other response worthy of my confounding and precious predicament. And though I continue even now to look up longingly into the sky and am filled with curiosity and awe as I consider the limitless planets brimming with other civilizations, peoples, and realms which I would all too willingly love to explore, I also look equally below my own two feet, and feel with a knowing sense that I am already out in that crazy cosmos, already an alien to others, already a voyager, at this moment stomping about on a beautiful and mysterious blue-green planet whirling out, and in, and through the universe where I belong and do not belong, and for that I cannot but bend down and kiss the ground of this wonderful, implausible, otherworldly earth.

*

118

two

I may have certain spiritual ideas not incompatible with conventional religion, but I am no evangelist. That would make me nauseous. Not that I have anything against evangelists. As a matter of fact, I find them quite entertaining, with their apocalyptic fervor, sweaty brows and armpits, and three-piece suits into which are stuffed their burger-turgid bellies. And, to be sure, I would much rather listen to one of those bombastic, bellicose men of God, instead of the soporific, and simplistic palaver of a new age guru, any day.

In fact, I once met an extremely unique ex-evangelist who came into my life at a very pertinent time, and though he bellowed as loud and eloquently as all the other well-dressed lightning wielders, he was neither well-dressed, well-behaved, nor even slightly charming, and, in a way, was an outright bastard. And yet, I stand and salute him, for reasons I will now relate.

I met Frank on the north shore of Oahu, during my time as a wayfarer, while I was chumming about with Geoff, the HIV-positive holy man whom I had met on my first trip to Hawaii. Geoff and I were sitting at an old wooden table in the sun, drinking our morning coffees with a number of other societal outcasts and street folk, and Frank arrived at our ranks with a larynx full of fire and brimstone, and began forcefully delivering his impassioned sermon composed of a hodge-podge of scattered axioms and novel platitudes. But Frank was no bible-quoting, mealy-mouthed preacher. He was the real thing. By which I mean that regardless of whether I agreed with what he had to say or not, and largely I did not, I quickly recognized that his ideas were completely his own, his observations were well thought out, his words were extemporaneous, and passionate, and his facts and proofs for his theories were based on no one's experience but his own. I had found myself a live wire, and I tapped in and enjoyed this rare breed of a man who had found within himself the fire to glow, and who came with a blazing torch toward anyone in his way.

Frank also seemed to take a liking to me, most likely because I did not agree with what he said, and I was none too shy to voice this, though nor did I snub nor disrespect him, and instead tried, as best I could, to dance with his character and energy, to create a thriving dialogue and transform his staccato monologue into a tête-à-tête where I could participate and surf inside with some flow.

We conversed for a couple of hours that morning, and then Frank asked if Geoff and I would be interested in coming back to his property and, for a couple of bucks, cutting down a few palm fronds from some tall trees, which he intended to use for crafts he was involved with.

Being ever low on greenbacks as I was, I readily accepted, and so we went back to Frank's place, and set up a twenty-foot ladder precariously against the palm trunks, up which Geoff and I took turns climbing, shakily and hesitantly, until we arrived at our prospective targets and hacked through a number of the fronds until we were finished.

Back on good old *terra firma* again, Geoff drifted mentally away, and Frank and I got to talking a little more personally, and after I shared with him that I was an aspiring writer, his eyes lit up and he beckoned me into his house.

There on a desk in the middle of his living room sat a stack of typed papers, rising about a foot high, which must have been no less than fifteen-hundred pages. His manuscript, a true magnum opus.

It turned out that Frank had been an evangelist back in Texas, up until about ten years ago, when things started going weird on him. He related that he began waking up in the middle of the night and hearing a howling, blood-curdling, terrifying wail from some animal he had never heard before, and it sounded ghastly, as if it was from hell itself, and was dying at the hands of a pack of deranged ghouls.

This sound recurred irregularly, every other night or so, and went on for a number of months, and Frank had no idea what was going on, and he was getting quite shaken, for the ghostly beast in anguish seemed to be getting closer to his house whenever the howling occurred. And then one night he awoke and the frightful sound was right at his front door.

Frank was shit scared, but made himself go to the door, and with the tortured groans wailing out in the night only a few inches from him, he finally found the courage within himself to open it, but nothing was there. Frank knew instantly where the horrid squeals of anguish had been coming from- himself; from somewhere deep within the caverns of his own soul's pain. And that was the end of his days as a conventional evangelist, and the beginning of his life as a man of God, or so he said.

After that meeting with whatever aspect of himself was in such sorrow and ache, Frank began years of solitude and deep introspection, and writing down conversations he was having with a voice he called Wisdom, the voice of God.

And there lay the fruit of his labors- fifteen-hundred pages of asking, listening, learning, and transcribing.

I spent only a brief period leafing through the papers, as I had no need to dive into them heavily, what with the living word in my presence, and though it would be impossible for me to sum up Frank's findings, a few key elements have remained that were the cornerstones of his perspective.

To begin with, according to Frank, although we are all, at this time, liars and thieves- and anyone who declares otherwise is also a self-deceived coward- although we are all liars and thieves, we are in this universe so as to mature, and learn not only how to live properly, but also how to create our own universe, just as Jesus Christ, who created this one, had done, and then died into it- as one must do as the final act which brings into manifestation one's creation. So saith the voice of Wisdom.

As I said, I held little agreement with this sixty-year old, four-time divorcee, foul-mouthed, truculent, recalcitrant sooth-sayer's opinion, but I liked him. Even if he were a liar and a thief and a self-deceived coward, I liked him, for he carried a boiling cauldron of enthusiasm and determination around inside of him, the force of which drove him on through life with a conviction and intent rare to find in this world of flabby-hearted followers.

Frank was no follower. No way. And that made me respect him. Though I also saw his imperfections, weaknesses, and confusions, and I even fell victim to one of his well-disguised foibles, after he had hired me to edit his manuscript and then pulled the plug at the last moment, exposing the bluffer hidden within. No matter, Frank was no follower. He believed in himself, in his own experiences, in his own words, and in his own creations, and therefore was true to his vision of this world, and the next. And for that I commend him, because, though I disagreed with his final conclusion- that we must die into our own creations- like him I saw that we exist in an infinite cosmos, not only physically, but metaphysically as well, and since we are co-creators of our life in this realm, I saw no reason why each of us would not some day have the skill, knowledge, and courage necessary to create our own reality, our own cosmos.

And therefore, I say, if Frank wants to die into his, so be it. I, instead, shall be born into mine.

I state these things without being facetious, because I honestly believe that God receives what God creates, and we are all pupils in the schoolroom of the master, learning that to be God is to create what we experience from what we are.

And though we are truly the only ones who can make or break ourselves, there is also a pedantic domain within the tenure of our unconsciousness; a rhapsodic impediment which obviates our ancient folly. There is a trembling underbelly buried beneath the mind of all men, a fevered and uncouth dominatrix pinned behind the eyes of the soul. And it is this imprisoned power which wails and gnashes in the night of all our days. It is this flightless monad, this empty revolver, this checked war cry which dooms us to become the victim of ourselves. But if that is the case, let me be instead the hegemon and not the prisoner. If I am to be held by nothing but my own force, let me wield that power and be healed.

121

I ask for this with both courage and trepidation, for I have seen many self-created disasters looming large in the lives and deaths of all who come and go from this plane, and I do not claim to hold the key nor the answer.

Perhaps this is why God once came to me, at a time when I was seeking to manifest something which I desired very much- but had not thought through all of its karmic and collateral fallout- and God asked if I was willing to take on the consequences of my creation, a question which set me aback and forced me to delve in and try to understood the gravity of such a power, and so begin to see that to make even the simplest of things in this world is to set an infinite string of dominoes falling, and to never know exactly what will become of that first push.

And so, until we are capable of creating what will not be disastrous for us to experience, we must remain under the tutelage of those who have mastered their means.

But when we are finally ready, we are released on our own recognizance, so to speak, and allowed to be the Maker and receiver of all that is Made.

*

three

Within a period of a year and a half I had danced with the making and lived in the made, and had spent extended periods of time in two of the places where Lemuria is suspected to have existed- New Zealand and Hawaii-, and in two of the places where Atlantis is speculated to have been- Santorini and Iceland.

I expect there was something in my nature, or something to do with my part in the greater show, which required me to mix energies in such polarized areas. Perhaps, because I sought wholeness within, I had to find wholeness without, and therefore I became as if a service vehicle, commandeered by my Godself, and driven unrelentingly to wherever supplies could be found to complete the cosmic stew.

Throughout those journeys, and the learnings which accompanied them, it slowly became apparent to me that to join the Mother and Father through ourselves is to allow Him into Her, which is to bring heaven down to earth. For when we invite the Father- Thy Kingdom come... - down to earth, through the lonely Christ within us, we become the conduit through which the Pater penetrates the Mater, and thus we reunite the cosmic parents, and, receiving both, become as One.

122

And though I lay no claim to anything other than my absolute ignorance in all things- for I am learning every day, failing every day, and being forgiven every day- marrying the Great Father and Great Mother within me would come, if ever it did, on my first visit to the sight of manifest creation itself- which is to say, at the pulsating, seminal, amniotic lava flow of Mt. Kilauea, Big Island, Hawaii.

I was taken out to the flow by two very large, very unique, and very gay men who I had been hanging out with for a number of weeks by then.

One of them claimed to have re-incarnated on earth so as to endure the trials required in order to receive his next promotion in the cosmic hierarchy- archangel status. This fellow was an eclectically brilliant sort, who at one time had entered into a sublime career for the spirit, in which he was requested to undertake a number of earth-energy related activities, including flying all over the United States one autumn to specific high energy areas, and, standing at the intersection of clogged Ley lines- the Earth's invisible energy meridians- he would empty himself completely and become a conduit for the energy required to repair the flow between them. He was an immensely entertaining, knowledgeable, generous and yet untrustworthy bloke: entertaining because he was full of ancient lore, mythical anecdotes, and new age theories, and was ever spouting these forth in effusive, theatrical joy, eloquently proffering all the fringe ideas which populate the esoteric world; knowledgeable because he seemed to know not only a little bit about everything, but a lot about most things, and therefore could draw laterally upon a multifarious contingent of oblique paradigms, and occasionally bring forth a juxtaposition which greatly impressed me; generous because he had fed and housed me for over a month when my poverty had become extreme, and had given me a haven when I needed it most; untrustworthy because he was forever seeking something behind his words, forever poisoned with the remaining fragments of his false ego, which made a mess of his genius, and forever utilizing his spiritual powers in hidden and devious ways, and therefore was a hypocrite who said one thing but meant something else, which is the last thing an archangel should be, since the first piece of knowledge such a being ought to arrive upon this earth with is the absolute realization that everything is clear in the sight of heaven. Everything. And therefore all thoughts contrary to speech are exposed to the hosts above. And the angels on high laugh with scorn and no pity when words come out of us which do not match with what is in our minds.

No matter. I saw his bad side and appreciated his good, and was better off in the end for his company.

The other fellow with us contended to have been, among other things, a Hawaiian holy man- a Kahuna- in one of his last lives. He had a great many spiritual talents, or so he said, including being able to diagnose a person's faulty 'trimeridian', which, according to him, was some such invisible organ in the subtle body responsible for, among other things, keeping a person's body temperature homeostatic. He also claimed to be somewhat of a psychic, crystal worker, massage therapist, and spiritual guide. He was a good lad, whom I enjoyed spending time with, though I paid little attention to his blithering, until one time when we were on the west side of the Big Island, and he was trying to convince me that I should be baptized in the ocean waters of a Hawaiian holy site which we were visiting. I told him that it was unnecessary, because I had already been baptized, to which he put up an argument, and was seemingly trying to guilt me out of myself, and so I turned viciously upon him and related, in not so soft terms, how he had no clue about what he was saying, because the baptism which Christ brings is a bludgeoning, and that he ought to stop prattling on with that pathetic chortle about how pretty everything became once you had been dipped in the sauce, because it wasn't the case at all, for when the Man comes after you, He comes so as to destroy you, and it is not an enjoyable event, and if you think it is then you merely betray your own ignorance. I gave it to him, and good.

Anyway, I still enjoyed his company as well, and had some truly remarkable times with both of them, even if they were simply megalomaniacs with outlandish and grandiose visions of their all too humble predicament of being human.

And so the three of us headed out late one afternoon, towards the lava flow, arriving from the little-touristed east approach, where we pounded a four-wheel-drive vehicle over the remains of roads devastated by Pele's last assault on mankind's feeble constructions- the Kalapana flow of '91- then onto an area of rough lava tracks made of softball sized chunks of the old Lady. Finally we had to park the vehicle and begin on foot, scrambling towards the shimmering wasteland where the living river of molten rock might be found.

We were out there about an hour and yet had found nothing except an endless field of dried lava. The sun was getting low in the sky, and it seemed our sojourn would come up impotent. And by that I mean that *my* initiation would not come to fruition, for, as one of my incarnate guides had stated- this was 'my trip', meaning it was my dance with the Mother, my chance to make connection, or not.

As the three of us stood there, deep into the heart of the solidified lava field, watching the sky darken, I was beginning to feel the sense of a failed project, of ships passing in the night, so to speak. And so I sat down, closed my eyes, and tried to make a connection with Her.

Well, it wasn't long before I realized that I wasn't going to make the connection, because I wasn't hearing or feeling anything within, and I could not pretend something was there when it wasn't. I was about to give up, call off the exercise, and begin the long march back, like one of Napoleon's officers stumbling haplessly across Siberia after the loss. But then a thought suddenly came to me- or was given to me- which was that the Mother needed *me* to participate, that I was necessary, and that my will was a part of our connection. And so I entered into stillness and humbly asked Her, if She was willing, to please create a flow about one-hundred yards out ahead of us. And that was that, and I got up and stated to one of my otherworldly chums that if the flow were to happen, it might be out ahead of us about one-hundred yards or so. Admittedly, I was full of uncertainty still. But at that very moment a light sprinkle of rain began to fall, and a brilliant rainbow appeared in the sky just behind us- the Father's covenant with me- and I let out a cheer I don't know why other than I knew then that I had been heard. And damn if you wouldn't believe it, but by the time we had walked approximately a hundred yards or so out in the direction towards which I had made my request, a small flow had begun bubbling up through the cracks of older lava, and widening out, oozing like dark, viscous lymph from the nipple of a prone woman. She had heard me, and had answered. And the Father, the Mother, and I were one.

Into that river of glowing liquid rock I spontaneously threw, as an offering, the straw hat I had been wearing for the last month, as I had nothing else materially to give than that hat, and nothing else immaterially to give than my identity- which the hat represented- and though I have said that Pele mostly desires cigarettes and gin as gifts, I gave all that I had to give, and, either way, when such a convergence happens, and you are a living part of a world so confounding, indisputable, and intimate, one which has run you through the mill for so long that the only thing you have left to offer is your individual identity, well- you do it, because you realize that there is no such thing as separation anyway, and therefore you only give away the illusion of your difference from the rest of life, of the universe, and of God, because the Son comes from the Mother and Father, and because you are unequivocally in and of the all, for which you are now a part that is not apart, and so cannot but scream out a glory and hallelujah by throwing yourself into the tumble and so giving back all you have been given.

The macrocosmic marriage takes place when the *sacred androgyne*, the Christ, is pulled between the Father and Mother- belonging to both- to such a degree that the individual dissolves as the bridge between them, and the cosmic unity is won. Is One.

When finally we are embraced by both the earth and the sky, at the very same time, we become the living interface, the writhing membrane where the eternal orgy between the opposed but not separate

125

forces of the Mother and Father- the yin and the yang- intermingle, and the Great Parents make love, and we are their orgasm creating the world.

Heading back home later that evening, one of my cosmic mentors voiced a claim, stating to me: "Now things will go easier for you", which they didn't. For, despite the magical union that night, little did he know that life is rarely easy, and that most successes usually lead to harder trials. But this is the type of understanding that unrealistic and overly optimistic new age types can't bear to accept, because it deflates their helium balloons and brings them back into the muck, the matter, the *prima materia*.

The Big Island is a vortex for such metaphysical types, be they delusioned seekers, or true visionaries. To be sure, that living chunk of rock in the middle of the Pacific, the Big Island of Hawaii, is a vessel whose gravity attracts and contains the most astounding variety of mavericks I have ever come to know. It is a microcosmic milieu of soothsayers, energy workers, medicine men and women, healers, dreamers, charlatans, quacks, queers, warlocks, and witches. It is a community of ganja smokers, ayahuasca journeyers, peyote imbibers, and mushroom takers. It is a land of Buddhist monasteries, Hindu ashrams, new age retreats, Mother Mary worshippers, Sufi mystics, and every occult genre under the sun.

The spirit runs so thick there at times that you can almost throw yourself effortlessly into its current, lose all plan and idea, and let the cosmic stream flow you out of your old pattern, whisk you hither, thither, and yon, and then set you down suddenly in another place, now more perfect for your part in the play that is your awakening to the dream of the whole.

*

four

A number of years after that initiatory experience at the lava field, when I had been away from the netherworldly isle for some time, I returned for a visit with my twin soul, with the intent to stay for two full moons. And so we arrived on the Big Island a few days before Luna's perfection, vagabonded about a bit, and then on the night of the full moon camped up on a high ridge, on the lip of the forested volcano located on the estate I had caretaken a number of years earlier.

That night we engaged in no ceremony or ritual- I do not believe in ceremonies or rituals- but enjoyed the clear sky, glistening stars, and radiant moon before falling to sleep in the wind and on the earth. Just as it should be.

We awoke just as the sun was coming up, and, turning around, we could see Luna's complete orb setting in perfect unison with the rising of Sol. This was a blessed omen, for a number of years earlier, on a deserted beach in New Zealand, we had experienced the exact opposite astral occurrence, while watching a full moon rise as the sun was setting. And so we had finally come full circle, had seen ourselves through a sublime cycle in which we had descended into the darkness of the earth's night together, wherein we had our many trials and misadventures, but then rose up together into the light of the sky. We had made it through the ambush of psychic chaos, and were now out of the discord of darkness.

All that had befallen us, and specifically me, over the years seemed now to be nothing but a result of a division which had been mended, and now new karmic dominoes were beginning to fall.

In fact, soon after that full moon, circumstances congealed into our meeting with a woman named Allanah, who was perhaps the closest manifestation to the Mother on Earth that I have ever encountered.

At fifty years old Allanah was the mother of five children ranging in age from three to twenty years of age. She had spent the last twelve years living directly upon the earth, under a large, palatial tarp- as many earth-children do on the island- where she cooked over an open fire, tended her garden and fruit trees, and gave shelter to those of Gaia's offspring who were drawn into her midst. I say she was living upon the earth, but it would perhaps be more accurate to say that she *was* the earth, for she was a truly incarnate aspect of the Mother Earth herself.

As soon as my mate and I arrived on Allanah's land I recalled a dream of perhaps six months earlier, in which I had been shown that area of the island, and had known in the dream that a very unique community existed there. And somehow, half a year later, through no effort of my own, I had been guided and welcomed to that very spot by the matriarch of the place. But that is the way of the spirit on earth, after all.

I was now on the Mother, and with the Mother, and it was not long before my own little microcosm in the macrocosmic play came full circle once again. And by that I mean that after a day or so at Allanah's, my twin soul and I were offered to caretake a nearby property owned by a man ...named Jesus. I kid you not. All is reflected through all. All is all. The actual is the myth, and the myth is the actual.

And though the Jesus owning the land was not Jesus, the Christ, still he was a man of generous being, and solid intent, and was by no means a scar upon the flesh of his namesake.

It appeared to me now that a lengthy chapter in the destiny of my life had run its course, and that the symbols of the manifest had mirrored back to me my awkward and imperfect journey, of courting the Mother, and serving the Son.

I was coming to see how truly involved we are in the creation of our own lives, how our thoughts and intentions play themselves out in both sublime and profound ways, and how the dominoes which I had set in motion, without knowing it, years earlier, had inexorably come to pass due to the karmic inertia of my own creative force. I say my own, but really I mean God's, whose Self is my self, and also is not, for we are the same and yet different, which is a problematic bit of illogic which I still cannot understand but have come to accept it as true, for this, like all contradictions, are part and parcel of a singular universe necessarily composed of dualities.

The world is my dream, *and* the flesh is my dream also. I AM both, and in accepting myself as being *and* non-being, I become the immortal self of this mortal world, for I am where flesh and spirit come together, and where the Mother and Father, who had been at odds, are now married and in harmony as they unite, taking each other into account, and making love through me.

The other is the same and the same is the other. The stable is the evanescent, the one is the many, and the coming is the going amongst all that remains. If the universe is built of opposites, then the ephemeral is proof of the everlasting. Though just as all opposites are dualities of the One, so too the transient and the eternal are each themselves two halves of an ineffable whole. To seek only eternity is to obfuscate that which is beyond the concept of time. What is always, and what is fleeting, are the yin and yang of a cosmic mystery so profound, so outlandish, and so subliminal, that it can never be found for it is everywhere, and can never be known for knowledge itself is one of its aspects. And so it is futile to seek, to study, to surrender, or strive, for all of these are mere fragments of what encompasses them, and is them. And so the striving, and seeking, and surrendering are themselves but grains of sand on an infinite beach lapped by an unknowable ocean, and the farther shore is the nearest place imaginable, which is why we can never find it, because the moment we look it is gone, because no vision can see itself, no wind can blow itself around, and no mystery can comprehend itself. And for that I raise up my glass and shout out Hallelujah! Hallelujah!, because the earth is, because God is, because I am, and because it is all beyond itself, beyond reason, beyond knowledge, beyond time, emotion, hope, wonder, duality, oneness, sex, love, creation, destruction, being, and nothingness. It is all beyond itself, and this is the glory, the perfection, the philosopher's stone: to finally arrive and be nowhere, to finally understand and be dumb, to finally bridge the incomprehensible gap, and so to become both the agonizing part *and* the ecstatic sum.

*

five

It was the interminable diversity of the community living in the area near both Allanah's and Jesus' land which provided a welcome stability which somehow grounded me. And in that grounding I was soon lifted off of the earth, and rooted in the wind.

It was a small community filled with an amazing assortment of diverse and individual souls. It was a spiritual community, though without any guru, temple, monastery, rules, orders, ideologies, or sacred books. Which is to say, it was a true spiritual community, for it had been formed sublimely by the spirit itself- just as with the collection of musicians I had come upon in Dharamsala, India- a fact which made God-the-Father the only guru, God-the-Mother the only temple, love the only rule, and life the only sacred text.

I had been guided home, or, at least, to one of my homes. For it was here that spirits and souls kindred to my own heart's longings lived in abundance, in varied locations in the area. Most of them existed in austere abodes, under large tarps, with no walls, only a basic kitchen area, a bed, some chairs, and an open-fire cooking pit in the center of their home. It was like visiting a camp of nomads who never moved, at least not on outward journeys, but instead had set out long ago on an inward course which would lead each one of them into the God of their own soul.

The folks whom I encountered there were a neverending barrage of delight and amusement to me. One such fellow named Tim had a great many tales to tell of his time on the mainland, while working amidst the dark spirit of the world. Tim was an odd fellow, to be sure, but one in whom I sensed a great deal of honesty and authenticity, which is why I enjoyed listening to his anecdotes- despite their oddity- about his habit of going into homes all across the land which had recently been the sites of mass murders, and sleeping there, and sensing and communicating with the tortured souls of the recently departed. It was as weird a hobby as I could imagine, and one which made me think Tim was a crackpot, and yet he held my eyes and did not seem to be lying.

On top of this absurd habit, Tim related other tidbits of his personal research and experience. He spoke of how the earth was ruled by a society called the 'Bonesmen', which was an elite group of men based in Yale university. He spoke of wars on Mars- those which had been and those which were to come. He claimed he had seen a person spontaneously combust, and spoke of personally being abducted and attacked by certain aliens, and of being healed by others. And lastly he spoke of his time as a roadie for the Grateful Dead, and of all the sublime spiritual events which occurred during the years that group focused the energies of thousands of souls into the vessel of love, freedom, psychadelia, and psychosis.

Another unique character I came across was a fiery, dreadlocked, genius renegade named Koosa, with whom I sat sipping wine one evening and who- in his own words- had died completely one night on an ayahuasca trip, died completely, and in that death learned that life and death are but one thing, and that death is simply a breather, allowing us to return to life rejuvenated, and- as I had found years earlier on one of my own mushroom journeys- that death occurs only when life in the flesh is no longer worth living. As well, during that trip in which Koosa had died completely, after coming back to life he learned about the necessary duality of oneness. And he learned this from a tree, no less, which told him that a female is like the roots of a tree, which are buried in darkness and would die if exposed to the light, and a male is like the branches, which must grow ever higher, and only towards the light, and that both the roots and branches are necessary, and one cannot live without the other or the entire tree would perish.

Next I met a woman living nearby who stated that she had met every president since and including Nixon, none of whom could meet her eye to eye. She claimed to have willed, and then been offered, an apprenticeship to be the anchor for the Today Show, but turned it down because she realized everyone in the industry was so unhealthy, an observation which she was perhaps qualified to make, because she had healed herself from cancer by forgiving a man who had abused her when she was young, and therefore had healed her inner anger. And after that self-healing she spent the entire following year eating nothing but ice cream and cake, and yet growing healthier, happier, and stronger all the while.

Yet there were not only these types of fringe oddballs running amok in the area. There were also absolutely sublime, peaceful, and wisened Buddha-types. One such fellow was John, a fifty-something father and grandfather, who had worked six days a week for twenty-five years while living on the mainland, and then had become divorced and lost everything, which he claimed were the best things that ever happened to him. When I met him he had been living on the Big Island for a number of years, making, selling, and playing bamboo flutes, living here and there as a caretaker, and enjoying the peace and tranquility of the earth, and, as best as I could see, entering into the inner chamber of his soul, without effort, without pride, and without care. In doing so he had become one of the most peaceful, non-reactive, fluid, and harmonious individuals I have ever met. And never a single word about spiritual or religious things. Nothing. He had arrived, and no words, nor ideas, nor pedantry could allude to the subtle realm into which his spirit had floated. He had become as if an epiphyte, which grows above the earth and not in the dark soil, and yet is as much a plant as any other plant, though it is rooted in the sky, and not tangled in the ground.

Though as peaceful and inwardly harmonious as John appeared, I was to meet with a young man one day who held an empty perfection and inner cleanliness that came upon me as if I was looking not at a being composed of flesh and spirit, but a window only, perfectly polished and without flaw, and which therefore had no interaction with anything, whatsoever. This young fellow had become the eternal, intermingled membrane of the invisible self flowing unmoved through the entire cosmos. And that is all I can say. For he and I met while in the presence of a number of others, and spoke only our names to each other, and then did nothing but hold each other's liquid stare for perhaps ten to fifteen timeless minutes, until a gentle smile crossed each of our faces, and we released each other from the harmony of that deep communion, and I have never seen him since.

It was in the presence of such a diverse group of souls that I found myself full of gratitude and acceptance, and in which I enjoyed a number of potent congregations that provided my life with experiences of spirit in community, the likes of which I had not known existed.

I recall one blessed gathering to which my twin soul and I had been invited, where an assortment of free individuals gathered to share spirit, song, ayahuasca, and healing.

As much as I had been filled with awe and admiration for my time spent with the group of musicians in Dharamsala, which I described earlier, that impromptu event in India had been but a trickling stream compared to the gushing river of life which poured this night through these people who had long ago turned away from convention and respectability, and had turned instead towards the earth, God, and their own eternal selves.

The evening was hosted by a man in his late thirties who had lived in remote valleys on Kauai for many years, had prayed and asked for guidance, and eventually had been led to the Big Island where he slowly built a life for himself out of cinders and lava, and at the same time he had created an invisible umbrella of spirit under which the community now gathered like a forgotten tribe who had not forgotten God's home.

To describe even a fragment of the characters attending the event would be to digress endlessly into the sacred precincts of three-score hallowed souls, for it seemed to me that I had come upon one of those anachronistic occurrences written of only in mythological or ancient tomes, because the entire collection of our spirits were released from our separative confinements by the medicine- as ayahuasca is called in the shaman's world- and we were then gathered up as one, into another realm, via the ecstatic music of numerous Sufi bards. For in attendance that night were a number of young men and women who had been called early in life to go to India, live in caves and with sadhus, and then take up as their spiritual vocation the art of the Sufi song. And boy could they sing. Let me tell you, I was in awe and gratitude while experiencing the overwhelming passion, grace, commitment, and talent I felt in this family of perhaps six men and six women, all sporting gigantic dreadlocks, heavenly countenances, and lithe bodies covered in flowing robes. And their music …their music was rapture itself. The songs went on into the early hours, and all souls danced in the unmoving ether, through the rapt presence of all who were one.

I had found a community to which I finally could belong. And yet, as is the way of surrender, I was soon being told in a number of dreams, that yes, these people were great spirits, and great souls, filled with immense faith, love, and service, and, yes, I would find myself drawn to these folks, and would accept and be accepted by them, and, no, it was not yet the place for me to stay. I was being told to live and love amongst them, and then to go another way.

It was the necessary repetition of this message, in a number of dreams, which helped me realize that though I cherished this opportunity to live in such a brilliant place filled with kindred spirits, there was yet another chosen spot up ahead for me, and were I to stay here I would surely find peace, freedom, harmony, and joy, but I would not fulfill my life's most perfect goal.

Following the spirit as such, over a number of years, I had finally come to learn one of the most important lessons of all- how to give myself completely to a situation, and how to let it go; how to invest my whole being into whatever lay before me, and then, to know when the shift was complete, to divest myself, to hug the ones I loved, to say goodbye, and then move on to other fertile ground. I had to learn to die only because it led to more life. I had to learn to let go only so that I could further receive. I had to learn to say goodbye, because only then could I say hello.

And though I know now where I am directed to go, I know not what lies there, but this, after all, is no longer a necessity for me. I say, let my Christ self be my inspirer, and I shall wander on.

For throughout the earlier dementia of my unbecoming, I had lost sight of the hard won reunion, and hid behind the shield of trivial whims, as life fell not loosely about me, but clung fast in wanton, false division. I had betrayed my sacred non-understanding by embracing a profane understanding. But now I had only the mystified acknowledgement of a stupendous, debilitating obviousness: awe and acceptance were the only responses I had left for being. For though mine was a distorted illumination; like the blinding light of the sun, bouncing off the lightless, light-giving moon, I did still rise up in the night of existence, and shine forth despite my subliminal darkness.

Ah, *blessed be Thy entanglements which complete me*, for it is Life's hand which moves me along, and I am but a reed in the flute of the infinite heart, a song of the generous voice which sings, and a dream of the fabulous Dreamer.

Divine orgy, profane delight. Fiddler, I am your fiddle.

*

six

The Christ is the center which is also the pinnacle, ever crucified into the new life, rising from the core of every plane, and pulling, like a great carpet, the entire cosmos upward. Like the topmost sprout of a growing pine tree, which appears as a cross, the Christ in all of us is the ever-changing form of an evolving humanity; the 'son of man' is the upward ascending yet earthbound rising newness, ever living and dying in, and as, the transforming flame of humanity's furthest reachings.

To be human is to be Christ, which is to be the intersection of the entire menagerie of visible and invisible realms, and to be bisected and constructed by the push and pull of these infinite, unique radiations of the cosmos. For the Christ is not a separate entity, nor is the Christ a separated entity, because the Christ is non-division itself, which is cosmic union, the marriage of all dualities. Christ is One, the Noah of now, carrying every pair of opposites across the tempest of spirit and into tomorrow. And this Christ is the absence which creates the whole, and therefore the Christ is the whole. The hole *is* the whole, which is the last stage of the microcosm, the last agony of separation, the last growth on the skyward tree. The blastema. The last to grow, the first in height. The first and the last.

And this Christ is not a person, for the Christ is the event of individual abdication of self-ownership, opening up into harmonious, sublime, undichotomized being, in which the unfoldment of life occurs synchronistically within and without the now unseparated individual, who is still individual.

Christ is the one within, who does not bother with mankind but trusts God in all things, which is the absolute surrender of personal interpretation, which is an offering that affirms "Thy Will be done",

133

which is the end of the ego. For with the utterance of such a statement a person becomes disinterested- they lose interest- for to truly say "Thy Will be done" eliminates the possibility of interest, for what interest have they now in matters? What's done is done. They let it be, and fall away, and are set free without having *done* anything.

As such perhaps there is no such thing as a saint after all, for miracles are performed in the saint's presence because of their absolute faith in the infinite possibility of spirit. The saint does nothing, but only abdicates his or her being, thus creating the option for divinity to occur in their stead. And that very abdication is divinity's first act, wherein the chastening flame descends so as to eviscerate the unlucky candidate through whom the spirit desires to operate, and thus the saint dies so that God can live. But also God lives so that the saint can die.

Redemption is thus empty, and yet full of sacrifice, for the closer you come to yourself, to the force which creates you, and to happiness, the closer you come to the possibility of true sacrifice, for then you understand the value of what it is you relinquish- the cost to yourself to acquire it, and the subsequent cost to release it. But you know also the psychic economy of such a decision, and why it must be made, and why you will make it, and why you will be the only one who will ever know.

Back in the pious and puerile years of my becoming, I had not only uttered "Thy Will be done" on numerous occasions, without, at first, knowing the absoluteness of what that actually implied, but I also committed a sacrifice, by offering to God something which I cherished, as a trade so as to benefit another who was in great pain at the time. That was when I came to understand very quickly the power such an invitation possessed, for I had given up something, something dear and precious to me- in an attempt to help another. I did so because, at that time, I could do no other. I had no strength to stand in the face of human misery. If someone near me was suffering, I suffered as well. I had no walls, and that made me a perfect candidate for Christ to come flying in with his shotgun and create all the trouble that was to come after it.

I believe that sacrifice, which I made without ever intending to ignite Christ's chastening upon me, was the key which unlocked the door to many of the events which followed. Though, looking back, I am not certain whether I performed any sacrifice at all. For since all and everything is an emanation of the One Godhead, nothing is separate, nor is possessed by a person which does not belong already, and firstly, to God, and therefore there is no sacrifice possible, but only a giving back what is not ours in the first place.

No matter, I soon found myself asked to undertake a number of endeavors which were always confusing and hard to follow, though I followed as best I could. What I gather from my learnings is that we redeem others by ceasing to exist ourselves. What I mean is that once we are in contact with God, there is nothing left to do but be absent, and thus let God do as God will. To serve the Christ, then, is nothing more than self-elimination, and deserves no applause, and no praise, because it requires no talent, no decency, and no honorable characteristics. I should know, because I am a sinner.

However, in learning about the new non-role which I had been bequeathed, I was beginning to understand why life in the world had been so troublesome, so hazardous, and so futile to me. I was beginning to understand the horrible truth about vicarious atonement, about how in our emptiness we offer a void to all who are full of anguish, anger, and woe, and in doing so we become their anguish, anger, and woe. This was something which I soon realized I was not interested in, and so I had to find a way to keep one door open, and the other door closed.

In the midst of mankind's confusion, I had to become like a one-way valve, empty and open to God within, and yet shielded and guarded against the chaos without; I had to let God out onto the world, but not let the world back into me.

That was the trick, to be like a physician in a leper's den- to touch without being touched myself. Because to let God pull another out of the claws of death, through me, meant to go down into their death without dying, and to care for them without caring for them. It was to hold a line between life and death, upon which to let God regularly descend and ascend, and slowly, ever slowly, coax them back up, while never turning away from life myself, never changing my direction nor stride but only for a second to stop, let God go down into them for a moment, and then climb back up while I was still living. Only in this way could they be whisked out of the clutches of the reaper.

For to redeem another without incurring trespass is to witness non-division with humility; it is to stand amongst them in your emptiness, to look them in the eyes without yourself, so that their God within can awaken, and their love can spill forth everywhere.

*

seven

In the descent of our spirits into flesh, we become aspects of the Father, entering the Mother, and so we bring Heaven down to Earth, and the Earth up to Heaven.

And just as He hosts spirits above, in the form of angels, archangels, cupids, and saints, so does She, who is the Earth, host

135

spirits down below, the company of which the Druids, Pagans, and any primitive peoples were as aware of as their own beings. I am speaking of the earth-spirit realm of animated matter, wherein dwells faeries, gnomes, elves, gremlins, and the living consciousness of trees and other plants. It is a realm still alive and thriving, and is a plane on which we humans would also be consciously dwelling were it not for the fact that we have cut ourselves off between the heart and the mind and have somehow exiled ourselves out of the natural realm.

To return to this realm is not easy, though not impossible either, for we are already a part of that twilight dimension, where all that is beats to a different pulse- the pulse of the Earth.

I have fallen into that fantastic realm in many subtle ways, on many different occasions, during my relapses into the other way of seeing, while out in the glorious natural world, and yet I have never so fully entered the Land of Pan as I did on two separate shamanic journeys which were catalyzed by the mystic psilocybin mushroom.

On one of these occasions my *soror*- my twin soul- and I had spent a winter evening on a beach near Vancouver, huddled under a blanket together while snow fell all around us, and in the quietude and openness of our communal vortex, we slipped into the nether realm and there together witnessed the forms of three laughing and naked female faeries, who were dwelling at the membrane between our two worlds.

Another time, my *soror* and I were out on a wild Pacific beach and we fell through the looking-glass and into the 'green realm', wherein we could perceive each other's earth-spirit beings, as well as the entire dominion of the earth's energy, bound in and through and of all living things. It is a realm to which we all belong just as absolutely as to the one we mistakenly call reality, for 'reality' is a misnomer applied by minds which have walked into an empty room, into a tight corner, and, standing with their backs to all else, declare that they have found the truth. Yet there is more than one reality operating in and of and through us at any given time, and it was during that shamanic journey on the wild Pacific coast, into the other realm, that I also perceived the discarnate, demonic force, now holding the earth hostage, and devouring and destroying Her. And this I say with absolute honesty, for there is a demon within the earth, perhaps within us all, which is enslaving, destroying, and killing the natural, living earth and its netherworldly creatures to which we belong and of which we are. And so it is only for us to give up our limited views and addictions to oil, electricity, buying, selling, having, and doing, and let our natural selves regain their rightful status in the collage of our beings, that we may again return to the wholeness of heaven and earth, spirit and flesh, and the marriage of God and beast which is man.

It is because of my experience of that dark oppressor causing

136

calamity upon the earth, and for many other reasons as well, that I now quite openly declare that I do not enjoy the spirit realm, and perhaps never will, for, compared to it, the material world is a holiday in the sun.

The spirit realm is thick and lousy with misguided entities, dark energy, parasitic spirits, and untameable ghosts. It is a realm in which souls are won and lost, repressions are given power, and courtesy is unheard of. It is anarchy, feudalism, slavery, monarchy, and the ever shifting sands of a plastic reality, all thrown into a tangled heap of intermingling wills and energies, creating a kaleidoscopic pandemonium stuffed inside a madhouse run by no one. And this is why I do not enjoy it, for I have faced many trials, many near disasters, many troubling moments, and odd encounters in that twilight frontier.

In fact, though the Big Island of Hawaii is paradisiacal, natural, otherworldly, and serene in many ways, there was once a time while I was on that living rock when the darkness of certain spirits was so thickly knotted into the drama in which I was involved, that I was told, in none too allusive terms, by the one who guides me, that there was an uncontrolled evil around which would end up harming me badly were I to not leave, and leave instantly, which I did. For I had learned by then that the Father of my being knows a great deal more than ever I have claimed to see.

And a similar occurrence happened in a remote valley in the Himalayas one summer when my *soror* and I were exploring the ancient Buddhist areas. We must have stumbled into a spiritual black hole, because all of the sudden I was in a terrible tangle with spirits which did not seem to have any interest in my well-being and the only thing to do was retreat as fast as possible because I was not capable enough of defending myself from such invisible, nefarious forces at the time.

Another episode occurred in Hawaii again, after I had seemingly broken a rib while body-surfing. I must have been invaded by a malevolent water-spirit at the instant of my body's impact onto the sand, because the pain in my ribs continued to increase as the weeks went by, instead of getting better, and I was wondering what was happening. As was my *soror*. So one night she asked for guidance and was taken, in dream, to find a small green woman who had somehow found her way into my body, so as to attack me, and was there gnawing away at my internal being until my mate ordered her with full shamanic force out and away and back into the sea, at which point the little green woman left, and the pain in my ribs began to slowly abate.

I was very thankful for my mate's assistance, and yet she was not the only one who had ever come to my rescue. Oh no, the number of times Jesus, the Christ, saved me from doom, when I was deeper in the darkness than I was capable of escaping from, were almost uncountable. In the past I have called upon the Man so many times that I worry of badgering Him. And yet, to this day I continue to call when the going gets tough, for though I am at times a coward, at least I am not a fool.

Ah, the spirit realm. Drop a gallon of liquid LSD into a small town's water supply, and you'll have a quick briefing on the chaos and disharmony I have experienced, and I know that I am not alone in this feeling.

One of the oddest happenings which occurred to me in the spirit realm came at a time when certain dominant aspects of my life were attempting to take full control of the wheel, so to speak. In this case, as in many others, my will and intent behind such a push inevitably exposed an unexpected energy, or spirit, attempting to intentionally obstruct me, or perniciously lurking in the shadows, for one pathetic or nefarious reason or another. It is astonishing how many desperate, destructive, and deceitful beings exist in this pandemonic realm in which all our spirits commingle, commune, and commit crimes.

The event of which I speak was completely idiosyncratic, unexpected, and hard for me to handle, and came about one evening when I had awoken from a dream in which I was being symbolically shown that there was some form of intrusion or intruder obstructing the furthering of my highest pursuits. Upon awakening in the middle of the night I remained in that pseudo-conscious, lucid state where the mundane and spiritual realms mix visibly. In that state I recognized a female spirit clinging onto me. She was not being aggressive nor evil, but soon I realized that neither was she planning to let go. That was when I understood- as such things are understood in that state, as in dreams, without proof or explanation- that she was the soul of a miscarried relative of mine, who had been lost before I was born, and so she had been holding onto me ever since I came through my mother's womb, so as to remain a part of our family. It was apparent that my spiritual pursuits and efforts had finally exposed her, though she had been hidden to me, and in me, for thirty-five years, and now had no desire to leave.

Nothing could be done to diplomatically persuade her to leave, and yet I was fully determined to extricate her from my being, for she was off of her own path, and encumbering mine. And, let me tell you, it was no small effort to pull her off and drive her away. She kept coming back with greater and greater tenacity each time I attempted to drive her away, and I had to dilute my care for her and give myself to the spiritual violence necessary in order to liberate myself from her clutches. This was all happening in the sublime realm, and when the ensuing battle was finally over I called on any spirit helpers available to come and guide her away from me and towards her own necessary

138

path, and new life, which they did.[22]

Yet as much as I am weary of the spirit realm, there is no avoiding it, for to exist, is to exist in the spirit realm, as well as many other realms, for all are intertwined at one level, concentration, or another.

The problem for me is that I have always been far too open, so much so that I suffered from terrible allergies, and neverending sickliness during periods of my childhood, which, I was to find out in later years, are sure signs that you are absorbing other people's negative energy, and becoming like the liver of the spirit, wherein all toxins are sent to be processed.

I was always too unhealthily open. As a child, at my grandmother's cottage, I often suffered horrendous allergy attacks, sore throats, or plugged nasal cavities, which could last for weeks, or even the whole summer. Many decades later I read in a metaphysical book that children who are very open often suffer the consequences- in the form of mental or physical suffering- from the pathos or corruptions of another in their midst. And there was one elderly person, living in my presence, who was as corrupt as they come; outwardly giving but inwardly taking, outwardly full of pleasantries but inwardly a murderer, outwardly caring but inwardly conniving and oppressing, and I suffered in the atmosphere of that person's psychic chaos without a clue that it was not simply a bad case of hay fever, or a cold that would not go away.

Later in life, as a young man, I had a certain type of pain occur on one side of my neck a number of times, which came on all of the sudden, would stay for a few agonizing days, and then slowly fade away. I assumed it was the remnant of an old football injury, returning now and then whenever I slept improperly. This, however, was not the truth, for I did not know at the time that we call someone a "pain in the neck" for very accurate, spiritual reasons, though in modern days we do not recall the lucid understandings which this now colloquial phrase once held in years gone by when the dark arts were more prevalently understood.

It was not until I met a woman up in Alaska one summer who was a wild and cocky mother of two, and who claimed to be a witch, that I began to understand the nature of psychic warfare. This woman told me a number of tales about her escapades in the realm of attack and reception. One such story was about a personality clash she had with a woman at work a few days earlier, which ended in a subliminal psychic feud, resulting in the witch sending out hate energy into her foe

---

[22] For any reader who is interested in a much broader, and more expertly compiled exploration of the spirit-realm, I would highly recommend Sandra Ingerman's book *Soul Retrieval: mending the fragmented self*, published by HarperSanFrancisco, 1991.

who was soon bent over in her chair, in terrible pain, holding the back of her neck.

I expect the witch's victim had no idea what was going on. And neither did I, on numerous occasions, until I became wise not only to the adverse effects of my own openness, but also to the ways in which other people's aggression, hate, contempt, or inner turmoil can be sent out from their being and absorbed by anyone in its path, even if that person was not the intended victim.

On one occasion I was in a heated quarrel with a person close to my heart, but who was not exactly inwardly honest about their feelings, and though they were claiming to care deeply for me, at one point they walked behind me and I felt a shooting pain go through my back, as if I had just been stabbed, which I had, psychically. And so I also then understood the term 'back stabber' in a way I never had before.

My openness problems were magnified because, along with the unconscious chaos and separation carried about by the ubiquitous *hoi polloi*, there were also absolute and irredeemable scoundrels who, despite their polished, convivial outward personalities, had sometime during their life turned inwardly against their fellows, had let hate into their hearts and all the darkness, dementia, and disease- which inherently accompanies such a plunge away from the brotherhood and sisterhood of mankind- in. These pernicious characters were almost impossible to avoid and root out from my life because their malevolent thoughts and feelings were kept well disguised from the rest of my companions who allowed, or even invited, these troglodytes into our gatherings. This was troublesome for me because I was, as usual, far too open to the psychic realm where love and atrocity mingle, and the hate-deranged spirits would seep in and defile me almost instantly, and I would leave a party at the end of the night, in which one or more of the devil's minions had been present, with a sickly feeling from the osmotic contact with these fetid creatures. And then I would have to direct all my energy towards cleansing the vampires from my blood.

Occasionally, during life, I was so open that if I was in the presence of an individual who was battling with some sort of inner demon or the like, I would later, that night, dream their dream, and enter into their subconscious, shamanically absorbing their hidden agony, and then, without knowing how, I would get rid of it. All such things I never intended, and when I realized such events were happening I made a stern vow and evocation to the universe declaring that I refused ever again to take on another person's sin, karma, suffering, or illness, for I was like a psychic whore with both ankles tied behind my head, helplessly allowing all who cared, to walk right in and screw me. And when that goes on and on, you end up like a spiritual sewer, with all the waste and darkness that people cannot, or will not, work through and discharge of their own accord. Some call this type of experience 'vicarious atonement'. I call it being clogged by mankind's failure to mature, and I refused to allow such things to go on with me any longer.

Not that I wasn't responsible for my share of the tragedy-of-the-commons. Oh no, I certainly grazed my untamed psychic bulls out onto the overburdened fields of the common soul as well. I am no saint, and have never claimed to be.

After all, as I see it, to become a saint or bodhisattva, is a catch-22, in that a soul attains such a level if, and only if, they are willing to renounce their personal liberation for the sake of all others. And therefore liberation, for the saint or bodhisattva, is not possible without this sacrifice, though nor is it possible because of this sacrifice, for they must be willing to lie down in the River of life, so that others may step upon their back and advance another pace towards God.

I must not, therefore, be a saint nor bodhisattva, because I am not willing to lie down.

So be it, I am not a saint. A saint serves mankind. I do not serve mankind. I serve God, the innermost self. I serve God because I refuse to serve mankind. A saint is like a female Husky, in the far north, who lies down with turgid tits on the frozen tundra and nurses the little pups. A person of God is one like a dog on the sled team, who pulls God onward, driven by the whip and the love of running. I am harnessed to the God who loves freedom. And so I lead without leading, and would die of hunger were it not for God, though without me God would freeze. And so, like a Pegasus towing the chariot of Helios, I surmount the heavens in service to God, the innermost self, and this is a matter of choice, and a labor for which I am ever grateful. But at the end of the day I, who am harnessed to the spirit, need my meat, which God gives to me so as to keep me strong, and which God takes from me so as to keep me hungry. As is the requirement.

*

eight

I relate all of these things not out of the presumption of knowing or understanding anything. I do not know. Let that be my fiat. And I can explain things no better than I have already imperfectly tried. No matter. To serve the spirit is an event beyond explanation, beyond fulfillment, beyond truth, beyond falsehood, and beyond right and wrong. And if the reader thinks that I am merely grandstanding through all of this, let them remember that I have declared myself a sinner, and not a saint. Though if ever I was a saint, it was an afternoon long ago, on North Beach- a thirty kilometer stretch of uninterrupted sand on the north end of the Queen Charlotte Islands, off the coast of British Columbia.

I arrived on the Charlottes and hitched up-island to North Beach, where I spent a few days walking and camping along that massive stretch of sand that is a membrane between the two worlds. And I strolled upon that lengthy wasteland more alone than I had ever been before in my life, and as far away as I had ever been from others, for I had said goodbye to humanity. I was finished with society. I had walked away, because I could no longer endure the inexorable loneliness and agony I could not avoid witnessing in the world.

After a few days of this I sat down one afternoon and the tears began to pour out of me because I saw what would happen to them, what *was* happening to them- my people- and how impossible the situation was. Nothing could be done. I had left, and left for good, and I screamed with an anguish like Demeter must have suffered when Persephone was sold out from under her into Hades. I wailed like an astronaut who had lifted off from his moribund home planet, heading out to where he knows not, and looking back as the fires raged on, engulfing his old world and everything he cared for in the unstoppable flames. I was not in Heaven, but nor was I in Hell, and the thought of my brethren, toughing it out down there in the bowels of imprisonment was enough to take me down and flagellate my soul. Oh, I begged God that day, begged God to do something, to help them all, somehow, because I could not endure the thought of everyone's lonely confinement, each in a glass cell facing all other glass cells.

That afternoon I wept on and on because of the agony which had no end, and which it seemed others weren't even aware of but which devoured them in every act, and every thought, and every minute of the day. And I had walked away from it, because I could not solve it, nor heal it, nor could I face it any longer. I cared too much, more than what was healthy, and more than I could endure. It was the most painful afternoon of my life, so much so that the memory of it even now brings a glossy coating to my eyes.

You see, that day when I cleansed myself of the entire earth's woe and agony, of all the useless human misery I had witnessed throughout the years, which came thundering down upon me, and I lay there between great gobs of tears, begging God to do something, anything, to fix it, by whatever means, because anguish and loneliness were everywhere, and I could do nothing, and there I lay broken open to the heavens, growling out beseechment to the sky, for I had, throughout the frantic course of my merciless chastening, seen all I needed to see, thought everything I needed to think, and sacrificed all that I had- you see, I knew at that moment that ...God heard me, and

142

God understood.

It was too much. Far too much. And when the day was over I walked back into the forest as if I had died and then risen, cleansed of a burden I could no longer carry.

But that was a long time ago, a time when my heart had no defenses, a time when I couldn't stop feeling what I couldn't help feeling, a time when I wanted to fix everything that I now want to see crumble, a time when I sought to help others while still needing help myself, a time when the Father had me by the throat, and the Mother had me by the balls, and only the strength of my heart prevented them from tearing me in two. But I was not strong. My strength came from my weakness. My love came from a lack of poise in the face of another's agony, my hopes came from not accepting what was hopeless, my prayers came from a lack of faith that all was as it should be.

I see now that it is the Christ within us whose heart weeps for human suffering, and so we must be careful that the sacrificial lamb does not become a scapegoat, for, to be sure, a person can die of grief, as I almost died- once for the world's pain, and once for my own.[23]

And what I was to find after that emancipating release of stored-up agony, of worldly pain which I had sponged into myself and then had purged out through bitter tears and woe- I found that the trick to living upon this earth without being taken down is to love yourself, but not at the expense of another, and to love another, but not at the expense of yourself, which is to have compassion without empathy, which is to love and yet be free.

For now is the time we must learn to be re-born in Hell, to live in Hell, and to not be in Hell.

I became free of much of what I was carrying back then, and later on I was to become freer because I realized that most people did not need nor want freedom the way I needed and wanted it. Strange, but true. Indeed, like some prisoners of concentration camps in the Second World War, who, it is said, upon having the chance of certain escape, chose to remain where they were rather than face the uncertainty of freedom, I encountered many people happily dwelling in cages that had long ago been torn down.

That was when I learned to leave each to their own loneliness and sorrow- for it was their lesson, their way, and their only chance of

---

[23] I can say that at one terrible point in my life I believe I had fallen victim to cancer. Never was I diagnosed by a doctor, but I had many intuitions and dreams that things were not well, and had three close friends, from half-way around the world, contact me during that time and tell me of dreams they had in which I was in great trouble, or dying. I believe I was dying, because of sorrow. And I believe that I was healed because I made the decision to love life. And that is that. Sorrow will kill, and joy will save.

return- and I should not bandage the bloodletting, or the worm would never be gone.

Indeed, I learned to stop trying to relieve misery from people's lives when I realized that they got out of life what they needed, what they deserved, or what they wanted, and, in fact, that much of their anguish was God-given pain.

And so, I had to clean myself out, and only myself, open up, and break down the walls which separated me from the rest of the miracle, though at the same time I had to cease letting others inside me, had to cease taking on their sin, and so block their anguish from devouring me internally. For once I had shed my skin, I found that others could easily crawl within.

That was when I took my white wings off, and put my black armor on. That was when my love turned from a feather into a sword. There was no other way.

To be sure, it happens to all of us eventually: you come innocently into life, laughing and playing and clowning about, the world pushes you forward, the days blend into years, everything appears to be reasonable, actual, and true. And then one rainy afternoon you stop suddenly in the tepid process of the day. You sit gently down for no reason. You stare into the senselessness of it all while the tortured miracle of life blurs away before your trembling eyes. And you begin to weep and weep and weep from all the hidden fault and pain, and you wonder why the hell it is the way it is, and you do not know, and it's all gone, all of it, and the whole show has the numb, eternal ache of a phantom limb you never knew you had.

But when the tempest has passed on, and the wind blows the clouds into sun, the implausible absurdity and miracle of life then suddenly cascades like benedictions down upon your fallen soul and an unknown smile is born within which flips the madness over, lifting you up agog and howling. That is what happens.

Indeed, until you have laughed yourself silly from loss, you have lost nothing, and neither have you laughed. For it is only then, through the critical gloom of becoming, when the impotent conciliations run turgid, and the swollen vein runs dry, that the folly may begin to delight itself, and that is when you begin to laugh, and laugh, and laugh, and not even know why you are laughing.

*

nine

I look back now and wonder if Christ had been trying to contact me for many years, beginning in my mid-twenties, until finally I awoke to the communication. I say this because, going over all the events which have transpired, and trying to put the pieces together so as to see what the entire puzzle is about, I recall having had a number of dreams, years ago, in which a young girl, whom I had known as a youth, named Melissa, kept showing up, and seeking some sort of interaction with me. I had no clue at the time why she was suddenly appearing in my dreams, and it was not until a number of years later, when much clearer contact had been made, that I finally deconstructed her name: Me Issa. Issa was what Jesus was called in Tibet. [24]

And though my interpretation of the Melissa dreams may seem a slight stretch, many years later, and just a year or so before writing this book, I had a dream in which Joseph Campbell came to me and said that after the crucifixion Christ had gone to Tibet. And since that time, Christ has come to me in dreams and made it apparent that I should no longer be living on the path which I was previously on, and I should instead move towards the more eastward aspect of my being- my oriental self. For it is only in the dispersion eastward, after the long, focused march in the west, that the soul dissolves its won consciousness back into the neverending One.

Which is to say, after our work is done, and we have completed our outward voyage, tacking effortfully into the wind, there comes a time when we must turn about, throw up our spinnakers, and, running with the wind behind us, set our course for the void of Self called home. And therefore, it was only after my concentrated dance along the western way, that I had next to turn eastward, so that the last aspect of God to be separated from God- the Christ- would eventually rise and be returned to the whole.

And though I look back now as one reckoning with all that has come to pass, perhaps I have not yet finished with anything at all, but only just begun.

I suppose this is a necessity for an occidental, like myself, to further the growth to wholeness of their microcosmic self, just as an oriental individual might need to seek out the western way later in life,

---

[24] This kind of interpretive conclusion might seem outlandish to anyone not intimate with their own subconscious, but often I have had dreams in which a person appeared simply for the use of their name. For example, a friend of my youth named Carm often appeared in my dreams when I was being told something about my karma; Paul Newman occurred occasionally when a new beginning was occurring for me- a new man was arising; and so on.

so as to balance out their metaphysical polarity, so to speak.

In the end, anyone who can find all opposites within their being- the male and female, east and west, good and evil, above and below- that person's self becomes the entire universe, and then there no longer is a self, only a clear and limitless banquet through and of and in which their consciousness, now the same as the cosmos, remains calm in the surfeit and silence while awakening within the dream. It is an awakening devoid of arrogation, of realization, of accomplishment, of pride, of joy, of sorrow, of nostalgia, or expectation. For it is an awakening to the night that hides within the day, and the day which lives within the night; an awakening where moon and sun consciousness merge beyond distinction into the quiescent realm where all elements are as if one; an awakening where water, air, matter and fire are distilled into a singular substance and song, where essence and form become each other, and the doingless doer is everything and none.

Which is to say that such a person ends up in a sea of absoluteness which is never the same, for it is always changing, which is the hard part to understand about absoluteness: it flows.

It is in this newfound realm where I have breathed like I have never breathed before, where I have apprehended as I have never apprehended before, and where I have belonged like I have never belonged before. It is here, in the presence of absent veils, and inside the transparency of liquid objects, that I am awakened as the stillness within and through and of all, and all is the awakened stillness in and through and of me, for stillness is the core which is no core. It is the marriage which is no joining. Because at the absolute center, in the stillness beyond time, there is neither recess nor distance, but only a singular, infinite space wherein the entire cosmos persists as a phantom penetration writhing through the impervious, immoveable space.

In that space where matter and consciousness are contiguous and the Mother and Father are one, the awakened self is that still essence forever embracing the manifold show.

Where the vertigo of infinite emptiness holds aloft the plenitude of exigent forms, the great absence suspends all presence, in and through and of itself, it is there that I dwell beyond myself with you who are no other.

And since finally there is no difference between God, the Earth, all others, and me, I lie down within myself, and flow into the never stopping movement, because I have stopped distinguishing what I am from what I am ...not.

*

146

ten

I wonder now if life only asks of us what we ask of life, if life only wants from us what we want from life, and if life only gives to us what we give to life. It must be so, for the whole of life is the quintessence of intimacy, the epitome of reflection, and the paradigm of reciprocity. There is no separation. Show me separation, and I will show you bonds as thick as the universe itself. We are in and through and of this great, incomprehensible madness born in the womb of our own disbelief.

And I wonder if God asks only of us what we ask of God. For though there is gain in serving God, to be sure, there is certainly also loss. And so in serving God one must accept loss. For how can one give of themselves without having something taken away? To choose one path is to kill an infinity of other paths. This is the agony of intent, and also its power.

I had to realize that if I did not accept that there is loss in life, huge, gut-wrenching, tear-your-hair-out-in-chunks loss, as well as heart-breaking missed opportunities, irrevocable blunders, torturous failures, manifold griefs, agonies, and sorrows- if I did not see and accept that this is as obvious and incorrigible as the sun, I was sure to be crushed under the weight of life's failings, instead of being lifted up by its miracles.

To think of the number of times I watched a lover walking away from me, or realized that a chance of inspiration or growth had passed right in front of me and then out of reach, is enough to bury me beneath a sea of sorrow as deep as the ocean blue. But I could not let loss win. I had to accept loss, and all the bitter thoughts that came with it. I had to learn to turn aside from every avenue which I could not take, and to not curse at my limited dominion. I had to come to terms with what it means to make a decision, one decision, and to understand why the root of the word *decide*, means 'to kill'. For just as sui*cide* is to kill the self, and homi*cide* is to kill another, to de*cide* is to kill the infinity of possibilities which will not be chosen but only missed, and mourned, because to decide is to look in one direction, and to never look back, and to know that this is necessary and unavoidable, because without making a decision and holding to it, life is filled not only with missed opportunities, but also with woe and ennui.

In and through the roundabout, fantastic, labyrinth of this cosmic tangle, I lost far more than I care to relate, but in that losing I found the one thing worth finding- my own eternal Spirit.

Along the way I roared because I had to roar, I danced because I had to dance, and I wept because I had to weep. Because I was also caught in being, and I hated it, loved it, wondered at it, and suffered it to the fullest completion of my soul. I dove into the deepest darkness I could bear, and flew to the highest summit on which I could stand.

But in order to serve my own existence, I had to destroy, to disorganize, and to go mad, for there was no other way to complete the necessity of my being, within the claustrophobic structure avowed to our life.

And so I became what it is only possible to become when the opposites of contempt and mercy, thought and feeling, and anger and succor come to exist with equal intensity within an individual- when a person comes to fully disdain life, and yet praise it as glory, without ever contradicting the One. Which is to say I became ...a human. And I became such for no special reason but that I began to care ...with ruthless love.

For a human knows how to stand alone in the midst of a lie. A human knows how to laugh when others are weeping, and to weep when others are laughing. A human knows how to believe in no one but him or herself, and so to believe in all people. A human knows how to forgive him or herself, and all others, and so to finally be capable of forgiving ...God.

A human knows how to accept and reject, how to affirm and deny, how to be different and indifferent, how to fight and how to surrender, how to dive to the deepest depths to retrieve a retrievable soul, and how to let another drown.

And a human knows how to be a man *and* a woman; to be whole; to descend into, occupy, inhabit, and become the rose of their own life and flesh. To be and to not-be, and thus to be two in one and finally free; to let the receptive, concavity of their being unvex the sublime pleroma, and to bring forth His convexity only in order to protect Her.

It is through this sublime androgyny that the circle becomes complete as the soul and spirit unite in splendor.

This sort of metaphysical tripe is not exactly the type of pretentious pedantry that I care to write about, but I have little option, having chosen to say it like it is, and let the critics have their banquet.

You see, I could do not but rise up from this punishing plane. And man I rose up like a phoenix scared out of its wings. I rose up, bold and mad from the challenge, the need, the impossibility of it all, and went forth into the dark and the terrible, with nothing but hunger and breath to carry me through.

I rose up not because I wanted to, nor because I knew where I was going, but because, beyond my wildest imaginings, I saw a truly horrible vision- I saw that nothing would change unless ...unless I changed it. It was up to me. No one could save me but myself.

I had realized that I could depend on no one but myself. And, still more so, that I was weakened by mere association with most others; that if I, of my own accord and volition, did not step out of the tide of mankind's folly, if I did not look hard inside and find out who I was, and why I was born onto this earth; if I did not with all my might seize this improbable miracle, I was doomed to never be nor know what was intended for me.

The only one who could save me was myself, and for that a gigantic, relentless effort was needed. I saw this fully. I breathed in, swallowed hard, and quivered only for the briefest of moments at this burdening realization, and after a single instant of masochistic acceptance, all equivocation vanished; invigorated by the impossibility of our tangled predicament, I grew strong, turned my eyes irrevocably into myself, and without courage or fear fixed hard that stare which would never again blink, nor weary, nor die, for I had chosen to hold and to make my own ground, to find and be myself in the hurricane of our ubiquitous confusion. I was on my way.

Originally, you see, I had found an entrance and mistook it for my home; I confused the doorway with the castle, and lived wretchedly in the foyer of mankind's interpretations. Then one day- by grace it was- I found a hammer, lifted it with my tired arms, and went forth savagely into the pain, the lies, and the folly, and I have not yet stopped from smashing. Wherever there is a wall, there is open space behind it.

The only way I found to break through was to learn to feel. The only way to feel was to kill the mind; to weep, to laugh, to scream, to punch, whatever it took. If the mind continued to hold the reins, the battle was over, and it was an easy battle to lose because when a man's heart is finally levered open by the jaws-of-life, the first thing he feels is the pain of all he has lost up until that point- lost without knowing how badly it had hurt him. The next thing he feels is the wretched sorrow and contrition within himself for all the pain he has caused others without knowing it. And it is these first two acts in the inaugural opening of the heart which often wreck a man who has never before allowed himself to feel, for the feeling which comes first, if ever it does, is a deluge of all the pain that has been repressed throughout life, in an initial torrent which will not abate until he has felt it all and transmuted it into acceptance. And that can be a great deal longer than a mere forty days and forty nights in a tempest.

Though were life suffering and nothing but, I would easily have remained apart, and never sought to descend. And yet I could do not but come down. Fall and rise, rise and fall, forever grasping through the thorns for the roses.

That there are roses in this painful life, and that I, like all others, try, but can rarely grasp them, that is our torture and folly.

And yet we come down only so as to find what roses we can and then rise back up again, up from the profane, through the mythological, to the divine- from the linear contextual, to the symbolic

149

contextual, to the acontextual- transformations through which we gather and disperse our fragments in a wholly unpredictable way. And so, by contracting and expanding our living nothingness ...we become the all.

We all start at the center, and we either explode or fizzle out. If we think or care too much we are finished. Which is why I say it is time for us to dis-solve, to forget ourselves into stillness, to suffer neither knowledge, nor judgment. It is time for us to become innocent again, to go mad, to live without knowing what it is to live. It is time for us to seek nothing, find nothing, run free; *time for us to be kids again, to play in the dream of life.*

It was in this way that I became Life, but it was a wild and unconventional path I walked, learning that every real decision was left up to me, and to me alone: to spit in the face of absurdity, to live completely in the freedom of the day, and to find my own true being. For in the end there was one Law, and one Law only to which I was bound, and that Law was ...to be Myself.

It had been a splendid metaphysical intoxication which had hemmed me earlier into being, an unharnessable freedom which roamed about my cage. And then finally, through that dynamic haze ensconcing every moment, I found myself dancing- yes dancing- in wild, blind ecstasy, through the mad and drunken night, to the rhythm which I alone heard, and which no other heard above their own.

Dancing the dance called life. The beat and love rushed through me, the flesh gushed pain and joy from the memory of the untameable soul.

You see, it was essential that I find a way for myself out of the agony of time, and the only way to do that was to find the rhythm of eternity within myself, where neither past nor present nor plans held sway, but only the peace and ambitionless miracle, swaying gently in the warm breeze on the farther shore, a shore towards which I swam with desperate abandon, into that thundering chaos of beauty and delight.

I was filled beyond repair, and emptied for the heart to heal despair. The rules had been erased, the truth was long deceased, now it was my turn to fuel the fire of madness and release. I was returning to the land of rapture and awe, lifted out of life, away from the term of our exile, by the very force which had sent me there. I was going home.

*

eleven

I am neither an apologist for, nor a proponent of, the use of drugs or purity as catalysts to assist a person upon their path. To each their own, that is rule enough for me. And though I have occasionally partaken of stimulating substances, as it were, I have also often abstained for long durations, and during those periods I was always startled to be beckoned by the spirit back into imbibing one or another of the invigorators.

As such, while staying on the Big Island of Hawaii, in that little, plywood hut which Brendan- assistant to the millionaire- had originally granted me, which was in a quiet, alternative-living subdivision, built on top of a lava field, just a few blocks from the ocean, and about a mile from the libertine beach, I had slowly eased into a peaceful, unhurried, and drugless inner calm, which had come about because over the few months of my stay there I had been moving to the tune of no clocks, no itineraries, and no rhythms other than my own, and so I had truly entered into my own personal rhythm, and therefore had begun to settle also into the rhythm of my most inward, eternal self.

Apparently, however, I was not yet as calm nor inward as was required of me, for one night I had an odd dream in which I thought someone was saying, in French, "Ça va, Ça va." I awoke quite perplexed, for I had no idea what this statement had to do with me at the time. And, furthermore, although I had a number of francophone acquaintances, and had studied the French language in the past, I was by no means a master of the language. In fact, on one of my trips to France I had walked about for weeks without a clock or watch, and when I needed to know the time, I would approach a gentle looking Parisian and, pointing to my wrist, inquire *"Quel temp fait il?"*, to which I received a great many absurd or condescending looks and responses, which struck me as odd, since I was only asking for the time, I thought. Little did I know that for three weeks I had been pointing to my wrist and asking what the weather was like. *Quel idiot!*

Anyway, I was unable to interpret the "Ça va, Ça va" part of the dream until I went to a local market later that day and immediately ran smack into a stall selling CavaCava, the Polynesian plant, also known as Awa, or Kava, the root of which is ground into a powder and made into a drink, and has, it is said, amazing soothing and calming qualities. This made me think that the dream was suggesting I try some, which I did, later that afternoon, brewing up a thick tea, and then sitting alone in the quiet of the tropical forest, where I slowly eased further into myself than I had been able to attain over the past few months of idle nothingness.

151

In fact, I was in such an immensely still, immaculate, and yet fully conscious state that in short time I had disbelievingly recognized the subtle division within myself, and within all humans- the division of the 'I AM' into the 'I' and the 'AM', which was a startling revelation, because it meant that my 'self' was actually a binary amalgamation of two almost autonomous halves: the discarnate, insubstantial, creative 'I', and the incarnate, manifested, created 'AM'. I was the 'I', expressing the 'AM', which I also was, and both were needed for me to feel 'I AM'. It was profound and disturbing, for now my self belonged to two separate realms; I was the two and the one, the whole and the divided. And I had a sense at that moment that most people live their entire lives thinking that their 'AM' is their whole 'I AM' and never stopping so completely within and without, that the subtle self, the true 'I', is recognized as the unmoving motivator that it is, and the 'AM' is recognized as the moving, materialized half.

To be sure, when everything else falls away, only two things incorrigibly remain: the 'I', and the 'AM'; the ego may be gone, all hope might be obliterated, all pleasure, understanding, desire, pain, and memory may be finally scrubbed off the plate, but the Self and its expression endures. Which is to say, the 'I' continues to perceive itself undeniably, and it also continues to release the image, or vehicle, of itself, the 'AM', the manifest beingness of its unmanifest non-being, onto the plane of matter.

I also sensed then that the 'I' and the 'AM' were somewhat at odds not only within myself, but also within the whole world, and this was the cosmic separation of the Mother and Father aspects of the Godhead. And it was now necessary to attempt a permanent reunion between them, which would require the Self to take dominion over both, and that would require the rare and complex marriage of two separate elements, the male and female, the mind and body, the 'I' and the 'AM'.

I sensed that there was an unavoidable tug of war going on between the two sides, as the gravity of the form sought to pull consciousness into the world, and the emptiness of consciousness tried to suck the form back into the void.

I understood then why there is such strife and division amongst families, friends, couples, and countries- because the division causing the conflict exists right within us, and is only manifested outwardly as a mirror for our own inner lack of wholeness. And it was only going to be through a superhuman union of essence and form, of light and darkness, of the 'I' and the 'AM', that the tension would end and peace would prevail.

I had found the cosmic chasm within myself. But, more importantly, I had isolated the two disparate sides, and only later did I realize that this is actually an essential step in the work. For only after the one is divided into two can the two become one again, and in a much more perfect and complimentary union than before. In this way the consciousness, the male, must become separated from the body, the female, before the two can be rejoined into one. That is: from the 'I' being contained in the 'AM', a disassociation must occur in which the 'I' separates from the 'AM', and then the 'I' must grow to contain the 'AM'. Now body is in consciousness, rather than consciousness in body. The seed within the soil has grown into the world tree, and now surrounds the earth.[25]

A person is thus 'established', as the mystics describe, when the conscious and unconscious, the spirit and the flesh, the mind and body, are no longer mutually exclusive antipodes, but are instead integral and not dichotomized. That is when an integration occurs through which both the spirit and the body become new; the tangible is now intangible, and the intangible, tangible. Thus the inside reflects the outside, and the outside reflects the in.

This diamond-body exists outside of creation and destruction- which are symbolic and diabolic counterparts- because it is now complete. And therefore there is nothing more to create, and it is impossible to destroy. The individual is now beyond the duality of time, individuated, established, and eternal.

But before the diamond-body comes about, the individual must find all dualities within him or herself, must accept and then transcend them, must be both male and female, good and evil, creator and destroyer, and so be neither of the opposites but a new and inviolable, non-contradictory aspect of the living whole. Then this aspect must also be released and the self must dissolve into the whole. For it is when the diamond-body condenses, and then explodes, like a subtle supernova, that the microcosmic aspect is sent like an infinity of crystal seeds throughout the rest of the cosmos, so as to join and be grafted and grow within, and as, the entire whole.

To turn the lead into gold is to become the sun in the stone, for

---

[25] Whereas Descartes produced the quintessential male axiom of "I think, therefore I am", in times to come perhaps humankind shall also embrace the quintessential female axiom, "I feel, therefore I am." And only when both of these are embraced will wholeness result. For to say that one is conscious 'of' being, creates the separation, for in a perfect union consciousness *is* being. Yet in each one of us the division is created by consciousness not wanting to be as slothful and limited as being, and therefore consciousness has not the courage to accept the intimacy of being, yet nor does being want to be as intangible as consciousness, and therefore their oneness goes to pieces. Hence the male 'consciousness', and the female 'being' within each one of us must accept each other as dual aspects of a singular whole, thus inviting not only the internal marriage, but also external harmony in relationship, and union of the microcosm with the macrocosm, self with the Self, and Being with Consciousness, for Being *is* Consciousness. This union infuses 'dead' things with the livingness of mind, joining dark matter with the will of the light.

that is what gold is; it is the light of Sol in the darkness of matter, the spirit in the flesh, the Heavens within the Earth.

To be gold is to be solid light upon the Earth, as immoveable as a cast-iron man, and yet as fluid as a sea of liquid metal; to be the same as the all, and yet distinguished from it- a moveable, indestructible, and yet ever-changing aspect of the great canvas onto which all life is painted; a flexing, flowing, and amorphous mercurial entity, able to assume all forms though possessing none, able to blend in and belong anywhere, though belonging to none, able to fill and complete an emptiness, or to vacate and unplug a void. Spirit and flesh, light and metal, gold, and yet not gold- the *sol*-id aspects of Sol, now come to settle in the structure of matter, and therefore to vivify the moon caught in the gravity of Her own lightless being.

Just as quicksilver is both solid and liquid, metal and molten, formed and yet free, to become the coagulated light of gold, is to bring the Father into the Mother, and to grow from the Son to the Sun, and so to become as solid as a rock, and yet as radiant as the sky.

To turn that base metal within, into the glowing ore of God, is to protect your light with your own darkness, and so to be established, individuated, and inviolable, for now no breeze, no consciousness, nor will can shake you from your goal and station, for you have become yourself, and the world's ways part like phantoms in your wake.

Beyond all contradiction and division, neither rejecting, nor accepting, I stand in the midst of it all, and am it all, and I am nothing. I am Self, no more, no less. All that is, all that I am, all that shall be or was, beyond and above, within and below, never leaving, never staying, always happening without cause, meaning, nor hindrance. I am found without looking, known without knowing, and felt without love, loss, nor pain. Basking in the boundless sea of consciousness, I gain nothing, for I am everything, I lose nothing, for I am everything. I permeate but do not understand. I exalt but do not applaud. I wonder but do not ask. I love but do not care. I give, but do not offer. I expand, but do not end. In the Unknowable Void of our eternal, magical beings- I AM. In the absence of attraction and repulsion ...I AM.

I the Creator. I the Sustainer. I the Destroyer. I the Cause. I the Effect. I the Beginning. I the End.

I the Dreamer. I the Dream. I the Immaculate. I the Delusion. I the Purity. I the Filth.

I the Word. I the Flesh. I the Revelation. I the Retort.

I, of the manifest and unmanifest. I, of the change and unchanging. I, of the abstract and contextual. I, of the feeling and indifference.

I, of the player. I, of the witness. I of the earth. I of the sky. I of the You. I of the I. I of the Eye. Eye of the I.

Divested from the thought structures of mankind, I have

entered into the pristine bridal chamber where naked beingness and naked non-beingness dis-recognize their differences and are unified into One. I am the all and the everything. I am life. The seen, and the scene. All of it. The whole damned, marvelous mess. And we are the same being. There is no division. None.

Find me. Hold me. Release me.

There is no self but self. One being, we are all One being. When you say I, I am that I you are. Only you and the world complete me, for truly I tell you- I did not know myself until I let myself become you. It all comes down to that- I am you, and you are me.

How distant and yet how near we really are. Breathe in and be emptied. Exhale and be filled. Swim in the sameness between us. Weep and I shall suffer. Laugh and I shall smile. Sing out, and I will hear you. Reach out, and I will feel you. Look out, and Eye will see.

I am the rain forever falling, the river forever flowing, the sea forever receiving, the mist forever rising. I am the absence inside the Presence, the space upholding the form. Oh, Spirit in the manifest, ether in the stone, I am the Life in all things. And I am laughing.

Find me. Hold me. Complete me.

*

twelve

Like Orpheus returned to Tartarus with the painful memory of love lost, we have all come down to retrieve our bodies, to swallow them back through the heart's warm hollow. For we have mortally descended into the bowels of humanity's confusion only so as to climb back out again on the divine stairs of disgust, concern, indifference, and ...wholeness.

The lost and abandoned soul wanders about on earth, never really touching down, never really belonging, never completely joining in, and therefore never assimilates its earth-self, until it happens upon its homeless home, finds familiar wanderers, marries into all of life for one brief moment, and then rises back out more complete and fulfilled than if it had spent its whole life in the air.

For it is not so much that we must seek to transcend existence, but that we must first descend into it. We are already above, the only thing left is to dive.

Thus we come down only so as to go up higher. We descend only so as to ascend. We fall only that we may learn how to eternally fly. For the only way to learn how to fly is to leap into the darkness below.

155

Climb as high as you desire, but you won't get your wings until you fall without crashing. Fall spirit, fall. It's the only way to learn how to fly.

For it is only through this world that we may come to grow above it; what does not put down roots, shall never climb towards the sun. No seed grows toward the sky, without first germinating in the dark and perilous tribulations it will eventually no longer call hell. For like seeds which first must leave the loving light, we suffer as we descend into the darkness- we struggle to blossom in the mire. Oh, there is no vision in the black soil; the seed buried beneath the cold earth shudders at the confinement as it begins to grow out of itself. It knows yet nothing of the sun, and even less of the heliotropic self ...it cannot help but naturally become.

When the spirit fully descends into and inhabits the flesh, liberating the slumbering consciousness trapped in matter, that is when there is no longer a driver and a vehicle, but instead there is a dance. For the awakened flesh-consciousness, the voice of matter, the Mater, is now in concert with the spirit, the Pater, the two are operating as one whole, joined in wedlock, united and without distance, and separation has become togetherness.[26] Then there is no such thing as Male or Female, there is only Self, for all opposites are relative, based on a point of reference which, if it disappears, they disappear. Thus we must lose relationship to all, so as to identify with all, and so to become all.

And it is only in crossing into absolute physicality where I have found peace, a peace which is the harmony composed of what is and what isn't, of flesh and spirit, of body and mind. By becoming both I become another, sitting still, and descending my spirit into the flesh, and holding it there, inhibiting consciousness from leaving, and so bringing about the yogic union so harmonious in its peace.

Oh, the mind may convince itself that the flesh is not real, but the flesh knows that it is real, and, in fact, the peace which the spirit seeks in all its rootless flying about is found only when it finally joins the body, because true peace is *in* the flesh.

Only then, after the spirit has entered the flesh, can the flesh escape to the spirit. Only when we let God in, can we go out- out like a flame being engulfed by the fire, for we rise up only when we finally learn how to breathe under water.

You see, we are in the flesh so as to redeem the flesh- to

---

[26] As in the Gospel of Thomas (#22), where Jesus stated that you would enter the kingdom of spirit: "When you make the two one, and when you make the inside as the outside, and the outside as the inside, and the upper side as the lower; and when you make the male and the female into a single one, that the male be not male and the female female..." This is the point where there is no separation between being and consciousness: being *is* consciousness.

absorb pain back into the Great Love. And we must remain in the grave called this world until the death it has died knows that we cared, and thus it comes back to life. Things are different than they were before; now it is not up to God to save us, it is up to us to save Her, the Mother.

We are here to be in the flesh completely, to exalt life, not to hide from it. If we do not return willingly from the deep absence, who will?

Just as the female Fig Wasp tears her own wings off in order to climb into the fig where she lays her eggs, so too the Mother has sacrificed her freedom to create us. Though She need no longer be confined nor ravaged by the Dark One.

As She pulls us down, we raise Her up.[27]

And so, as the Piscean era comes to an end, and the Aquarian age arises, I see that the line running down into the depths now slowly reverses direction and, and after climbing towards the surface, ascends above us, and instead of catching human fish, it now tethers a rising kite.

And I see that the *Pieta* has shifted, and the Son now lifts up the Mother. And so now we cast our lines above us, and ourselves be taken up. For were the kite not tethered to the ground, it would not play so freely in the air. And thus we all shall eventually be lifted off of the earth by the same parachute upon which we have fallen here, and so our roots shall be wings, and our wings shall be free.

Unseparated in this way, we will become the common ground of all, for it is only through our love of the Earth that we shall set Her free.

To love Her, and to stand firm and angry in that loving, and so to take Her with us.

To love. To rise.

To take Her with us.

*

---

[27] The Adam (atom) enters (i.e. 'falls' into) the Eve (event) in the lowering of energetic vibrations, changing from the fluidity of pattern (Pater) to the solidity of matter (Mater).

thirteen

I am the self within the Self, the microcosm within the macrocosm, the smile within the God. I have been in this realm for what seems an eternity now, and though I am weary and worn, still I must complete the greater will, for when the fullness of our cosmic complexity falls helplessly into your lap, there is little to do but rise up stoically and follow it. I followed, like a blind puppy, nursed on the milk of the ether.

My true home is an opulent marble castle sitting by the great waterless sea, wherein anyone who belongs is given a great house of beauty all their own.

My sword is of quicksilver, my armor of air.

When I breathe, the Great Mother inhales me, when I sleep, the Great Father dreams on.

There is no wisdom on this earth for a man like me. *I am myself. That is wisdom.*

Between the profane and the divine, lives the psychic, intermediary realm of myth and symbol. Here all opposites meet, intermingle, and go to war together. Here is where the non-existent forces of Good and Evil actually exist. Here is where the individual is most constricted, and yet has the most effect. Here is where my people are trapped, laughing and weeping, and running about.

Here it is also where one, seeking to rise up from the profane to the divine, can get caught forever in the middle ground- between the tug and pull of the two waters, so to speak- without knowledge or hope of a further redemption.

It was down into those lower waters where I descended, and where I had a vision of old men casting nets from the land into the shallows, the intertidal zone, a place where, hours earlier, there had been solid ground. And now I saw that the fishing was good on the fertile patch where it was sometimes ocean and sometimes land, where the spirit came and went, and where God left it to man to stand chest-deep in the flowing chill, and harvest the ebbing keep.

And so, taking on the flesh like a trout flailing half exposed in the shallows of a rocky brook, did I come to live here, where it is not fluid, and where swimming is without ease, and yet I have grown and evolved in these partial streams, and it is here that I have struggled, and loved, and cast my seed. Here, where I have sought longingly for the combined elements of unreason and exaltation divorced from praise. Here, where I surrendered, vanquished, screamed, and then went dancing. Here, where I slipped and repelled those agonizing resonances. Here, where I was the string not struck, the chord not plucked, the silence needed to give rise to the harmony. Here, where I became no longer an ingredient, but instead a catalyst, spent in the reaction, and then left to the side to wait for another call. Here, where I tried to save God by a mad dash at His own throat. Here, where I sought to return the dying flesh to the living word. Here, where I found release from the senselessness of our keep, and the images no longer controlled me; here is where I bask before the lost and changing glory of it all.

I, who recover the Rose, time after time, from the tortured depths of the black, strangling hell of Hades; I, who link the archetypical with the actual; I, who eat only an unknown fruit caught falling naturally from the Tree of Life; I, who drink only early morning dew found settling in the navels of androgynous, sleeping angels; I, who have fallen into this realm like I have always fallen- through the stars, the sky, the clouds, through the mountains, buildings, trees, through the crowds, the noise, the laughter, anguish, dreams, desires, words, illusions, lies, and deaths; I am a man who knows nothing. I have come from the region of exasperation, in hopes that this world is prepared for my call.

My primary duty- as it has been explained to me, time and time again, by countless, cryptic voices- so as to serve my vision onto this myopic earth- is to be myself, my true self, and only that, completely, and at every moment. And though I have not come without struggle, and do not remain without pain, I now stand in the midst, and flow without meaning, for when the blood and tears have been washed away, and the time of ardor has spent its day, the truth of my sojourn shall become clear: Stand alone, victory man, stand alone, in the hour which does not betray you.

At the base of my past feverish existence has lain the eternal task of resurrecting the vast expanse of wonder, for it was there that I was fully sobered by the wild euphorias of my tempestuous incarnation.

If only people were more stupefied by the spectacular implausibility of their own incomprehensible occurrence. Oh, if only. Just once, Lord, let me make drooling morons out of well-appointed fools; better it is to lead a person into a larger prison, than to leave them bound because you cannot release them.

I imagine that no one wonders at 'being' as much as myself, and yet I despair at how little I wonder. And so I take in the jeers and applause, the loneliness and communion, the struggle and the surrender. I take it all in because that is how it comes to me. For life exists as a package. The extremes are limited only by the limitation of their opposites. The life more abundant explodes in every direction. I take it in, chew, swallow, and digest it. I assimilate life. The nature of my being does the rest. That I may puke, shit, or laugh from it is of little matter to me. I love life. It is this unconditional acceptance which is my victory, defeat, doom, passion, and glory.

And for this I can say, with absolute honesty, that this life we are given is limited only by ourselves, and that anyone who puts their heart into it can find their true soul mate, the Great Spirit of Being, Christ, Mary, their siblings on the Tree of Life, the Source, the Finish, Satan, God, and much, much more in this great and unpredictable existence we are in and which we are. It is all here, and it is waiting, and we are the only walls between finitude and infinity, and we are that infinity also.

For in my frantic peregrinations throughout the civilizations and wild lands of this earth, I found our famed Mercurius, the fair Nefertiti, the wild Poseidon, and the perishing Pan. I met and drank with the worn apostle Paul, and was hugged by the new and ever gentler Assisi. I knew those who could converse with animals, and others who saw the Living Light in day. I walked with Christ, was assumed up to heaven, met saints and angels in the ether, was kissed by Mary, coddled by the Mother Earth, and beaten occasionally by the powers.

I also became alerted to the ways of Mara, or Maya, or the Second Mary, as you will. My temptress, my illusion, my lover.

I roamed wild in the tempest of the archetypes, and held audience with the Myths and Muses. I sought wholeness and mercy for all, spoke with men of God, and with God himself on occasion, and let me tell you, life was still all implausible and insane.

I had taken a good run at the great divide I had to cross, and leapt with all my desperate might, but even then I was lucky for the unpredictable stepping stones along the way, and even with them I eventually had to swim in the river warmly meandering nowhere. Oh, let me say this, as the Mercies swelled to meet my sin and anguish, I fell short of the mark and yet was still gently lifted over the line. For as a parent easily lifts a child over a fence which would have been an impenetrable impasse otherwise, so does Christ take us across a line we cannot pass of our own ability. And that alone is why I made it across the desert and out to sea- not because I could leap well, but ...because I was willing to flounder.

And now I remain on this earth, as myself, dodging life's false responsibilities, listening for the as yet unwritten Word, that I might write it, and hovering weightlessly in between the gravities of two opposing forces, where I continue to survive the hemorrhage of false meanings, forging on to diffidently blaze a precipitous trail through the hazy, hallowed regions, of revolutionary exasperation.

And, to be sure, I continue to learn, to fail, and to be forgiven. For that is what happens in the re-ascent to our immortal selves, where there is no trial without error, and no salvation without sin; where fear eventually becomes loneliness, loneliness becomes acceptance, acceptance turns into faith, and faith leads to union; where confusion becomes revulsion, revulsion becomes indifference, and indifference turns into ...wonder; where reaction turns into action, action turns into inaction, and that ...that is when you become God.

*

fourteen

It is a deep and terrifying dive into matter which the spirit takes towards wholeness. It is a drowning and a rescue, a death and a transformation, a loss of breath and a growth of gills.

I can say now that I am as much an aquatic, as a terrestrial, arboreal, aerial, and ethereal being.

I am a whale, a snake, an ape, an eagle, a tree, a monster, an alien, a God. And it is only through the symbiosis of all these aspects that I also am a human, for humanity is the nexus, the crossroads, the hub through which all realms collide and commingle, which is why it is a crazy, brilliant, and disastrous thing to be human, because to be human is to be the pinnacle of the ever churning cosmos. To be human is to be Christ, which is to be the living tension consciously existing in all realms at once, and therefore gluing the entire disparate cosmos into a workable whole.

Yet, in the fecund rays producing us forever, how gentle it all becomes- to be human- as the separated blooms finally merge with our hard-won unlimited light.

You, who have landed here where I also came down into the quagmire stillness; here, where the pageant of being masquerades before itself; here, where the blossom falls into the fruit; here, where the shades of life are also life, and the grey dawn also knows the sun, and the gentle caress of the northern wind blows without asking if your tears come from shivers, or sorrow, or joy; here is where I came through suffering to gratitude, exalting what had deranged me, because I began to understand what was happening- somehow I had gotten back on track, I don't know how, but somehow I was returning to the source of gratitude, to God, to the mystery that I call ...me. For no one can know themselves completely, because the part is an aspect of the whole and a toe knows not where the walker is walking, and thus it surrenders to the whole.

To lose your part is possible only when you become it all, which is to become nothing. For a complete equation must balance out on either side. And therefore when you become it all every birth creates a death, every smile a tear, every pride an awaiting humility, every sin its forgiveness, and every piece of wisdom contains some ignorance. To become it all is to stand outside the contradiction, beyond character

161

and magnitude, at the wellspring and stasis of this infinite nothingness.

It is that void to which I now return, when I am still and empty in the shower of the electric God-presence pulsing into what was me, and still is, though continuous now with what it wasn't, and therefore is the sex of God's penetration into the concave adoration I have become in my own absence; it is this union which becomes the apocalypse to all separative energies now caught in the wrath of our indefatigable love.

In that consummation of gyrating motionlessness, where the form has been tamed by the core, and the lightning held by the rod, the bridge between the two waters becomes their non-difference, and the transcendent deluge of the new essence infiltrates an active dispensation into the living schemata of the generative whole.

In that commingling Avalon, where the new Eden is born without time, need, nor meaning, and the shift through epochs now adorns the inimitable cosmos, I dance continuously in the unrepressed glory of our orgy, song, and redemption. Where the realms of sex and God, libation and liberation, eternity and change, freedom and love, separation and union have been reworked and configured into the new and everlasting model; where madness is as certain as joy, wonder as absolute as wisdom, blasphemy and prayer the same utterance, and peace as prevalent as ecstasy- this is the yogic union, where the spirit settles into the awaiting flesh.

Where the rhythm of eternity soaks in and overtakes the mitigations of circumstance, and the neverending Self becomes the ever thankful recipient of its own benevolent creation. Here I linger in the warm and tonic recesses, where the flicker fades to a gentle hum, the organs grind to a sigh, and all those who belong to me will ever know they are welcome in the place I have gone to which is called Home. I am home. Come home.

It is a place where everything is consciousness, and there is no inside looking out, for there is only attention; where the self falls into the great abyss of nothingness, and yet Being remains complete. It is a stillness without walls, where life blows through you, and you are a gust.

As if through a window you look out onto the world from a house, and indeed there is a window, but ...there is no house, there is only one wall, and no roof, and everything flows over and around that wall, so there is neither inside nor out; in fact, there is not even one wall, only a window, and there isn't even that, only a place which moves in the wind, and is the wind, blowing and being blown, with nothing to block or prevent it, and nothing which might enclose it, or hold it, or make it say 'I'.

Oh, let me tell you- when God's great eyes are finally inside of you, then shall you be still.

In that austere event- when the self is only 'I', or even less

162

than that, perhaps as nothing- it is then that I become the all, and more than the all, and continually more and more than that.

For there is only one soul, and not two, and our love is its love, our hate is its hate, and our life is it living. It is us- we are it. So there is nothing left to do.

You enter the presence through the absence, and the absence through the present. The spirit becomes the space within the flesh, and the flesh becomes the space within the spirit. The union is harmonized, separation evaporates, and the distinctness of two become an intermingled one. Non-being enters being without a ripple, effect, desire, or repulsion.

To be in Tao is to be the non-reactive self, ever aware within the reactive panoply.

As I penetrate the empty fullness with my essence unrestricted by the form, flowing out from, into, and through all that is, I merge with and become that which becomes me, as a dye released into a tank colors the entire water, and I influence and am influenced in the vast space in which all that is, and I, soften into one.

It is here that the indifference of my eternity heals the wounds caused in the separative calamity of our unfoldment. It is here that the molecular substratum of our sublime continuity shifts and shapes the new form into being. It is here that I and you express ourselves through the complete exhaustion of the cosmos, infiltrating without force the fluid pattern with our oceanic lives.

It is here that Eros and Agape shed dissimilarities, here where the hard parts become supple, here where the orgiastic union of spirit and soul climax without end in the blend of distinct frequencies harmonized into the rapture of Avalon; where all difference and effort end, and only the dynamic self-perpetuating dance of ecstatic co-creation pours itself out, through, and into all that it is. It is here that we come to the wholeness of our sexless, hermaphroditic universe, and our eternal lives reclaim their evanescent throne.

It is this quiet dominion, where King and Queen bathe in the mixing waters of their volatile song, where all is birthed without hindrance, through that uncreated epicenter, generating the expansive home in which all worlds unite, and all realms belong.

It is this subtle union, this effortless penetration, this ubiquitous pouring of the sublime self into the rigid world which brings the leavening quicksilver of spirit to the awaiting womb of flesh, and the hard knot of wingless matter is freed through its dissolution into the rootless wind of Self. All is in Tao. All has become fixed, fluid, fecund, and free. And the universe is won.

You see, as the vortex of being accelerated, and the angels gathered to fly, I leapt off into the whirlwind and ...I became the wind. I did not weave this integral, complex fabric of being, nor did I unstitch

163

it, I merely blended into patternlessness, became contiguous in the realm of all happenings, and then moved freely amongst its fibers. It was so bloody easy- I simply melted into the sublime.

Yea indeed, discordant frequencies converge in the chaos, and a wholly new harmonious sound can be heard. For in the end it is not so much about giving up the ghost, but of giving yourself up, and becoming a ghost.

Like the ash from a cigarette which holds its form after the burn, but has no form, and is dispersed away in the slightest of breezes, I was not swept into the sea, but merely washed away like a stain of blood upon the earth. I dissolved into the tide.

Be it salvation or destruction, of that I am not sure. In the end it seems there is no valuable difference. In fact, there was little holy or unholy about my destined ungluing, I simply melted into a solution of forgetfulness and completely lost myself.

A window, that's all I truly am, and not even that; I did not, as I had romantically hoped, see through myself to the great beyond- *It* saw through me.

Either and every way, the little drop exploded in the storm, and then there was no more lightning, thunder, nor rain, only the great sea of something free.

This is the absence which brings the great redemption.

Find your true nature, and the world will fall through you, back into the Great Love. Then into everyone's eyes in which you look, you will see only your own, and then it is as if you don't even exist, for God will look through you onto what God has made and ...even God will not understand it.

Then it is that you shall unknow in the midst of knowing, and know in the midst of the unknown. You will be nobody, and everybody, and your finitude shall be infinite. And in that holy, common, non-existent space between our two unseparate worlds, you and I shall dwell without dwelling, rest without stopping, and move without going on.

That is when what goes in is the same as what comes out- and 'I' is the meeting point. That is when I am neither inside nor out, but am the spaceless infinity between them; neither ego nor other, and yet both.

Thus there is no division where neither inside nor out exists for they exist as the One; duality unseparates itself and incompleteness reconciles the opposites into completeness, because whether *It* comes out of you, or goes in, you are still included. You are none of it, and you are all of it.

Yea, in the gap between the receiver of what goes in, and the producer of what goes out, lays the infinite nothingness in which ...I AM.

164

When I hold onto nothing, and let myself fall away from care and effort, easing into the hopeless surrender of my own omnipotence, that is when the self I pursue falls helplessly back into me from the vacuum of my ambitionless void. Everything becomes mine because I become everything.

It all ends and begins in such stillness. All of life emerges from, and dwells there. God does not see you, or me, or any others; God does not see many, God sees One. When the edge collapses the center grows, the hairy beast sprouts feathers, the feathers become flames, and the fire turns the chaff into manna.

It is a manic dawn which breaks in and rolls over and upon you. It is a glee and tremor which catapults you away to the here which is nowhere. No more repentance. No more concern. No more assurance. No more to learn. 'Now' has taken over and devoured you. And you have devoured now. Like the famed Uroboros, with the head of time eating the tail of space, engulfing itself to nility, and from that zero all infinities are born.

In that flagrant summation, from the stillness which does not accomplish, I welcomed myself without genius, and I remembered the Self without guise.

In the choiceless calm of uncertainty, I stopped without stopping, and forged on without moving an inch.

In the midst of being I forgot being, in the midst of life I forgot life, in the midst of myself I forgot... me. And so, through the delirium and sin of our earthly predicament, I fell, rose up, walked on, forgot and ...was innocent again.

As the specious forms dwindled in the new light of the day, I stood again before myself.

In the fallen throes of our august conundrums, the ebb and flood of enstasy and ecstasy merged wantonly at the center of my absent circumference, and I spun helplessly about until I was lost in the heart of the vacuum; I vaporized behind the sight I was seeing. Oh, I did not succumb to the fabric surrounding our great mystery ...I succumbed to the Mystery itself; I soaked right into the whole damned mess of it, and then I was no longer.

In that ubiquitous realm, void, or feeling ...I AM! In the coy equanimity of no gain, growth, nor loss ...I AM! Before the mirrorless mirror of my existent non-existence ...I AM!

Yes, yes, I know- this seems like hardly a cherished denouement. Yet there, in the tempests of unreason, there in the desertion of all hope, there, in the ethereal dance of emancipation and of loss, with neither volition, idea, nor rule ...I finished, but not at the finish; I walked on without walking; I ended, and ...I did not end.

*

Epilogue

There was a period in my life when I often said that I would refuse to come back to this world- that I would do everything within my power to finish with my karma and duties in this life, and be done with this plane for good. I refused to come back unless things changed drastically, because I had seen enough of mankind's sorrows, vanities, errors, petty pursuits, and worthless creations, and I had endured the misunderstandings, the incorrigible immaturity, the noise, pollution, desecration, false theories, pathos, and joyless joys. And, having seen society for what it was- a madhouse run by somnambulistic schoolchildren- there was nothing left to do but turn away with an accepting scorn, forget the world and its contortions, and sink back into myself, into the spirit, and the earth, and then fly away to another world, and let the mayhem continue on without me.

As I said, I was going to refuse to come back. But then, I thought, if I had to come back, I would be certain to return only as a trickster, like the great Cosmic Raven of the Pacific Northwest. And I would sunder mankind's world into ruins, and I would do it all with play and laughter.

Oh, the cataclysms would begin very subtly, with unnatural creations such as elevators and escalators suddenly becoming faulty, and so everyone who lived above the earth would have to haul their own flesh above it. But then the stairs would begin to crumble, slowly, ever slowly. No one would be hurt, not by me anyways. I am no murderer. But eventually all buildings higher than one floor would have to be abandoned, and these would begin disintegrating back into nothingness. Then the world's fuel supply would end abruptly. No more fuel. Nothing. Dams would begin to crack and then burst. No one would die. There would be plenty of time. Electricity would become impossible. Movement would be slowed to a governable pace. Mankind would have to return to the substratum of their own abilities, to the earth, and to prayer. And I would be laughing as the hordes roamed about in bewildered disbelief. I would screech with delight at the deluge of pitiful tears streaming down from mankind onto the wounded earth. And when it was done, and all was laid bare, and I had roared in ecstasy over humanity's gnashings, that is when I would swoop down like the great Thunderbird of old, and I would take humanity in my mighty talons, and for no better reason than the thrill and the joy, I would teach my new found fledglings how to rise up and fly.

But that is mere speculation. The reason I had desired to never return was somewhat complicated, but runs like this.

Firstly, there was a time in my life when nothing was easier than to fall in love, and falling is an apt expression. I have fallen in love so many times, with so many people- women and men alike- that often I did not even recognize that it was happening, for it was an aspect of my sympathetic nervous system, like my heart beating, or lungs breathing, it happened of its own accord, the moment my soul received another's true nature. And yet, secondly, and paradoxically, I had great distaste for society, and so I was falling love with individuals, and yet despising the herd. And for this reason have I loved who I did not judge, and judged who I did not love, for such dispositions within me are mutually exclusive. And as much as I have, with love, allowed others refuge in my spirit, so also have I driven them off with judgment, for that is all that is required to divide me from another; when judgment lies hidden behind the veils of the cornea, knowingly or not, then it is the winter of all souls caught within my separative gaze, and I hover at the apogee of the Antarctic heart, which may walk intimately amongst many others, but lives eternally without siblings, which is a fate worse than that suffered by the denizens of Dante's *Inferno*.

But then I realized that I disliked humanity mostly because I expected *it* to give me something, which was impossible, because that something I could only find myself, *within* myself. And so I lost a large part of my contempt for the crowd when I recognized that the masses could do nothing for me; that even if they gave their all they could not budge the ingot from its roost upon my back. And thus I began to be slightly amused by my fellow man, rather than slightly nauseated, knowing that we were now wholly independent of each other, and removed by a distance greater than the earth to the moon. A recognition which, although it gave me great loneliness at the time, also brought great peace, and a new sense of liberation, because now instead of thinking about how to fix the world, I was only responsible for fixing myself.

And so I realized that to condemn humanity was like criticizing a blind man for his inability to see. And who was I to pass judgment upon others anyway? Who indeed? I was nobody, claiming to have vision, which I didn't have, for in the last analysis I had only perspective. One perspective.

In fact it was my judgment against others which created much of my pain to begin with. And I had to accept that my reality was a limited reality among all others which compose the whole, and that if I accepted others' lives, humbly accepted them, then I would begin to see my own limitations and uniqueness in an even more profound degree.

167

For an orchestra is composed of many different instruments, and each must play their own tune if the music is to be complete. And it is the bricks which build the castle, not the castle which builds the bricks. And we ...we are but intentional partitions in the sidewalk, making the Way divided ...and complete.

And so, despite the perils of love, eventually I had to bravely re-open my heart, and learn again to see my brother in every man, and my sister in every woman, and so to love each person as I have loved these two.

This learning, it seems to me, is the quintessential rite of passage of the heart, for once we have loved, then we have lost ourselves into the whole, and then there is neither love, nor hate, nor struggle, there is only Life.

I am reminded here of a drunken street fellow I met in Honolulu one winter. He was panhandling outside of a store, and beside him was his older buddy who was in a wheelchair. I had come to the tortured tangle of the city only to purchase a flight to another island, and was trying to make a quick escape, but the hobo hounded me, and, after brushing him off at first, he and I fell into a gentle parlance while I was waiting for my bus to the airport. After a few minutes the bus was in our view and slowing down to stop and pick me up. I was about to part from the outcasts, so I bade them farewell, somewhat perfunctorily, saying "Take care of yourselves", to which one of them responded "We are not selves any more." This made me stop, and turn back and inquire "Then what are you?" to which he rejoined "Brothers and sisters."

Brothers and sisters. They had made it. They had realized that no one can separate their self from the suffering of the world, because separation is the suffering of the world. They had become members of the whole human family, had lost all desire or need to have more than any other, or to be greater than another, or to control, or impede someone else, and had descended, willingly or not, into the substratum of the common soul where all people are siblings. For in the end there is only one rule, one admonishment, one caveat in order to be considered fully human, and that is, of course, the golden rule of love.

I realized then the necessity of this earthly siblinghood- which Christ had understood so well- and how it is essential that we must see our brother in every man, and our sister in every woman. For the life of siblinghood is the love of all. And so to truly live- to be Life- is, in the end ...to be the miracle of love itself.

And this miracle is only possible because all life is one life; because we are all one flowing, evolving soul. One soul. All of us; we are dreamed of inside the same Dream, and until the timeless tide ebbs again in our favor, we are fragmented, yet we are One.

Anyone who sees this completely will never hate again, but

only love. Indeed, anyone who has love inside of them has few lessons more to learn in life- for they are Life itself.

Love is the absence of separation, and is beyond 'other'. To go beyond other is to go beyond 'me', to unite the opposites of inside and out. Love is that bond which redeems the flesh, for it shatters the vessel of separation, and lets the spirit flow through all.

And so to bring Heaven down to Earth requires abiding by the one law of Heaven, which is Love. Though this is not an imposed law, per se, because Love, by its very nature, *is* Heaven, and therefore those who love are in Heaven, and those who do not, are not.

And yet to come to this Love is both the hardest, and the easiest thing in the world, for to be love is only possible by being ...ourselves. For by being our true selves, with no lie, cunning, denial, separation, nor guilt within us, then nothing is left to prevent the love called God from descending into and becoming us. Nothing.

And for this reason it is possible to leave this plane only after we have loved all humanity, for in the living moment of love we cross over from the death called separation into the life of Living Oneness.

And so, if one day you have come, as we all must come, to weep scalding tears for the loneliness and misery of the whole world- if you can take the entire suffering and lostness of mankind into you, and if you can hold it, comfort it, and then release it- then the trial of the heart is over, and you can go on your own way. Once you have added your link into the chain which holds Heaven and Earth together, then you are free to go.

For when you are finished with the rest of it, you suddenly realize what love is, and how and why it is the only thing that matters, and the only thing that is real, and the only thing that will save you. And so you stop caring for anything else, and you begin to love, and your walls come down.

And you are saved.

*

169

"Go, love without the help of anything on earth."
William Blake

In, and Of : *memoirs of a mystic journey along Canada's wild west coast*

by Jack Haas

ISBN: 0-9731007-1-0

"...an enthralling, true-life account..." *Midwest Book Review.* "...a poetic and stunning piece of work.." Nancy Jackson (*Dog-Eared Book Reviews*) "... Read in awe." Benjamin Tucker (author of *Roadeye*)

The Way of Wonder: *a return to the mystery of ourselves*

by Jack Haas

ISBN: 0-9731007-0-2

"...especially recommended reading for students of comparative religion and personal spirituality." *The Midwest Book Review.* "...a most unusual, and powerful book." George Fisk (author of *A New Sense of Destiny*).

The Dream of Being: *aphorisms, ideograms, and aislings*

By Jack Haas

ISBN: 0-9731007-5-3

A unique compendium of poetic aphorisms, transformational drawings, and esoteric insights.

171